AF600491

THE CATHOLIC UNIVERSITY OF AMERICA
CANON LAW STUDIES
No. 363

THE MEDIAEVAL CONCEPT OF AN ECCLESIASTICAL OFFICE

AN ANALYTICAL STUDY OF THE CONCEPT OF AN ECCLESIASTICAL OFFICE IN THE MAJOR SOURCES AND PRINTED COMMENTARIES FROM 1140-1300

A DISSERTATION
Submitted to the Faculty of the School of Canon Law of the Catholic University of America in Partial Fulfillment of the Requirements for the Degree of Doctor of Canon Law

by
DONALD EDWARD HEINTSCHEL
Priest of the Diocese of Toledo

THE CATHOLIC UNIVERSITY OF AMERICA PRESS
WASHINGTON, D. C.
1956

NIHIL OBSTAT:

EDUARDUS G. ROELKER, S.T.D., J.C.D.
Censor Deputatus

Washingtonii, 15 Aprilis, 1955

IMPRIMATUR:

✠ GEORGIUS J. REHRING, S.T.D.
Episcopus Toletanus in America

Toleti, 18 Aprilis, 1955

Printed by The Abbey Press, St. Meinrad, Indiana, U.S.A.

B. M. V.
REGINAE
SACRATISSIMI
ROSARII
SCRIPTOR EX PIETATE

FOREWORD

When the Canon Law student of today approaches the study of ecclesiastical discipline as embodied in the Code of Canon Law, he has no idea of the complexities which his forebears faced in their studies. The Code in its precise legal terminology defines for today's students all the many institutes of law which took centuries of development to reach their present state of definition. To the law historian, however, these very complexities become a channel of intensely interesting study and research, daily increasing his appreciation of today's terse expression of the law as well as opening to him the keen juridical minds of the great lawyers of the past. All of this in no small way aids in the development of a true canonical sense so essential to a firm grasp of modern canonical science. All one has to do to establish the importance of a study of legal history in Church law is to read Canon 6 of the Code wherein is set out the role that the discipline of the past plays in the present legislation of the Church. The Church in virtue of its divine foundation has always placed great stress upon tradition, not only in the fields of Dogmatic and Moral Theology, but also in the field of its discipline.

It was with these thoughts in mind that we undertook this treatise on the history of one of the most fundamental canonical institutes, the sacred or ecclesiastical office. In the following chapters we have tried to derive the mediaeval concept of an ecclesiastical office. We have studied in some detail the principal sources and printed commentaries from the publication of the *Decretum Gratiani* (1140) until the closing years of the thirteenth century with the hope that this chronological analysis would illustrate with some degree of accuracy the genesis of canonical doctrine in this regard, and fix the concept of an ecclesiastical office in its mediaeval setting.

The writer wishes to take this opportunity to express his heartfelt gratitude to His Excellency, the Most Reverend

George J. Rehring, S.T.D., Bishop of Toledo, for the special privilege of being allowed to pursue post-graduate studies in Canon Law and for his generosity in making this publication possible. The writer also wishes to express his sincere appreciation to Stephen G. Kuttner, J.U.D., S.J.D., J.C.D., Professor of the History of Canon Law at the Catholic University of America, at whose suggestion this study was undertaken, for his scholarly assistance, for his continued interest in it, and for his constant kindness. He is deeply indebted to all of the other members of the Faculty of the School of Canon Law for their many suggestions and direction during the preparation of this dissertation.

TABLE OF CONTENTS

CHAPTER I

INTRODUCTORY NOTIONS

When Jesus Christ established His Church, He created two offices, that of the supreme ruler, the Pope, and that of his subordinates throughout the world, the bishops. When He appointed these rulers of His earthly kingdom He conferred upon them the powers necessary to fulfill the mission which He had determined for His Church, namely, to teach, govern, sanctify, and save all men. "All power in heaven and on earth has been given to me," He said, "go, therefore, and make disciples of all nations, baptizing them in the name of the Father, and of the Son, and of the Holy Spirit, teaching them to observe all that I have commanded you."[1] With the development of Christianity, however, these officials were unable personally to attend to this mission. Consequently, they fulfilled their task by sharing these powers with others, and so in the course of time various ecclesiastical offices arose.

Fundamentaly, a sacred or ecclesiastical office has a particular relation to the hierarchy of jurisdiction in the Church. Christ gave to His Apostles and their successors a twofold power, that of orders, for providing men with the supernatural means of salvation which He instituted, and that of jurisdiction, for ruling and governing men towards the attainment of their eternal destiny. By divine institution these two powers exist in the Church in hierarchies, i. e., in various degrees they are participated in by a special body of men known as the clergy. The hierarchy of orders is made up of bishops, priests, and ministers; that of jurisdiction is made up of the Supreme Pontiff and the subordinate bishops, but these two grades of jurisdiction, established by divine authority, have by eclesiastical law been augmented with others, which partake of their power in various degrees.

[1] Matt. 28, 18-20.

There are a number of differences between the power of orders and jurisdiction, but the one of chief interest here is the mode of acquisition. The power of orders is acquired by sacred ordination alone; that of jurisdiction, either by a properly performed deputation, in the case of the Supreme Pontiff, or, for all other grades, by a canonical mission, namely, a legitimate mandate of a Superior, the validity of which mission is regulated by the power and the laws of the Church. From this sharing of powers then arose the canonical institute known as an ecclesiastical or sacred office.

Needless to say, the constitutive elements of an ecclesiastical office have varied somewhat throughout the history of the Church. The purpose of an ecclesiastical office, however, has always been that of aiding the Church in the attainment of its end, namely, the eternal salvation of men. In practice, to determine what were the necessary elements and the extent of jurisdiction have posed problems for the canonists in the practical determination of what constitutes a true ecclesiastical office. In other words, it has always been difficult to determine in what way and to what extent a definite charge had to partake in the the mission of the Church to be classified as an ecclesiastical office in the strict sense of the term.

Immediately prior to the Code of Canon Law an ecclesiastical office was restricted to those positions which participated in the power of jurisdiction. Wernz (1842-1914), for example, defined an office in the strict sense as follows:

> ... est gradus quidem iurisdictionis ecclesiasticae quoad personas, causas, locum legibus Christi vel Ecclesiae in perpetuum ita institutus, ut iura et onera spiritualia ipsi adnexa nomine proprio et ratione quadam stabili sint exercenda.[2]

While a measure of jurisdiction was necessary to constitute an office in the strict sense, all that was necessary to constitute an office in the broad sense was that the charge have

[2] Franciscus X. Wernz, S. J., *Ius Decretalium*, (6 vols., Vols. I-II, 3. ed., Prati, 1913-1915), II, no. 240.

annexed to it the right of performing some act of orders or of administering ecclesiastical things.[3]

The Code of Canon Law, while retaining in the concept of an ecclesiastical office the essential elements predicated for it in the pre-Code law, extended the definition of an office, whether taken in a strict sense or understood in a broad conception of that term. The Code defines an ecclesiastical office in the broad sense as "... quodlibet munus quod in finem spiritualem legitime exercetur."[4] Hence the only requisite for an office in the broad sense is that it be a charge which is exercised according to the norms of law for the glory of God and the good of souls. According to this definition an organist, a sacristan, or other like persons must be considered to have an office in the broad sense. It is worthy of note that the incumbent of an office in the broad sense may be a lay person, since there is no power of jurisdiction or of orders necessarily involved in such an office, thus settling a perplexing question which had troubled the canonists of an earlier age.

The definition of an ecclesiastical office in the strict sense, as given by the Code, reads as follows:

> ... munus ordinatione sive divina sive ecclesiastica stabiliter constitutum, ad normam sacrorum canonum conferendum, aliquam saltem secumferens participationem ecclesiasticae potestatis sive ordinis sive iurisdictionis.[5]

As is evident from the definition itself, the concept of an ecclesiastical office in the strict sense has been widened to include also the case of a participation in the power of orders as a sufficient foundation for such an office, a harking back, as it were, to the jurisprudence of Gratian.

Technically, then, each office has its specific purpose. Each office carries with it definite obligations and is endowed with specific powers. But all ecclesiastical offices have this in common, that they are the seats of jurisdiction and admin-

[3] Wernz, *loc. cit.*
[4] Canon 145, § 1.
[5] Canon 145, § 1.

istration whence radiates that power which Christ gave to His Church for ruling and governing man towards the attainment of his eternal destiny.[6]

In a study of the mediaeval canonical sources one finds no specific treatment given to this concept. Rather, these sources speak profusely of concrete entities, as for example the office of bishop, archdeacon, legate, judge, and so forth, and deal for the most part in great detail with the many duties and functions connected with these offices, and most frequently identify these functions with the office itself. One may glean, however, from a more searching analysis of the mediaeval legislation and writings that this term had varied significations in the mind of the canonists. It was often used to signify the exercise of the powers received in ordination; however, it was also used to designate dignities, positions of pre-eminence, and even the exercise of simple administrative powers. The term, in other words, had a relative meaning only, that is, one which was contingent upon the context in which it was employed. For example, in cathedral and collegiate chapters there were dignities *(dignitates)* such as the archdiaconate—or provostship or deanship—which were canonries to which the right of precedence and the power of jurisdiction in the external forum were attached;[7] there were canonries to which the right of

[6] The term *officium* was used by the Roman lawyers in various ways. For example, it referred to the moral duties originating in family relationship or friendship *(officium amicitiae);* it likewise referred to the duties connected with the defense of another's interests *(officium tutoris, curatoris, advocationis).* In public law, *officium* denoted the official duties of any person employed in public service as well as the office (bureau) of a magistrate together with its personnel. The term was also applied to provincial offices and officials, and in particular to provincial governors. The first book of the *Digest* and of the *Code* contain a large number of titles dealing with the duties of various imperial officials in Rome and in the Provinces. Several jurists (Venuleius, Ulpian, Paul, Arcadius Charisius) wrote monographs "*De officio*" of higher governmental officials. Inst. IV, 17; Dig. I, 10-22; C. I, 40; 43-46; XI, 39.

[7] X, I, 6, 54.

[8] X, I, 25, 1.

precedence was attached without any power of jurisdiction, as exemplified by the *primicerii;*[8] and, finally, there were the "simple" offices *(officia)* or canonries which carried with them neither any right of precedence nor any power of jurisdiction, but simply the right to administer certain ecclesiastical goods, as for example the offices of sacristan[9] and treasurer.[10]

Ioannes Andreae (1272-1348), when speaking of chapters, reserved the term *officium* for those simple canonries which had annexed to them neither precedence nor jurisdiction; in fact, for him an ecclesiastical office merely involved the exercise of executive power in the administration of the *res ecclesiae.*[11] This, however, is not to be taken absolutely. Elsewhere the mediaeval canonists used the term *officium* to designate any ecclesiastical function, usually involving, although not in all cases, some participation in sacred orders.[12]

Another difficulty in determining this concept arises from the fact that the ecclesiastical institute of benefice was intimately linked with an ecclesiastical office in the mind of the mediaeval jurist. By the eleventh century the vast majority of ecclesiastical offices had been endowed with some source of revenue. Although there is a clear-cut and precise distinction between these two institutes in modern legislation, this was not always true of the past. Frequently the terms were used indiscriminately. In the early Middle Ages an office without a benefice for its incumbent was practically

[9] X, I, 26, 1.

[10] X, I, 27, 1.

[11] "... tamen proprie ista tria: dignitas, personatus, et officium differunt: nam dignitatem proprie dicitur quis habere qui habet administrationem, et cum hac habet iurisdictionem sicut abbas ..., sed personatus dicitur is habere qui in ecclesia habet aliquam praeemenentiam, non tamen habet iurisdictionem sicut ille qui in ecclesia, in capitulo, et aliis honoribus praecedit canonicos; officium vero dicitur quis habere qui sine iurisdictione et sine praeemenentia habet administrationem rerum ecclesiasticarum, sicut est sacrista ..." *Glossa Ordinaria*, ad I, 4, in VI°, in principio.

[12] D. XXV, 1; X, I, 2, 8.

non-existent. In the following article, therefore, a brief consideration will be given to the development of the canonical institute of benefice.

Article I. The Concept of an Ecclesiastical Benefice in the Middle Ages

The traditional definition of an ecclesiastical benefice worked out by the later Decretalists (16th-17th century) is thus stated by Ferraris: "... est ius perpetuum percipiendi fructus ex bonis ecclesiasticis ratione spiritualis officii personae ecclesiasticae auctoritate ecclesiae constitutum."[13]

As can be seen from this definition, the concept of a benefice can be approached from two viewpoints. First of all, when one considers its principal element, one would define it—as does the Code, but not the early Decretalists—as a sacred or spiritual office established by ecclesiastical authority to which office is attached the right of receiving an income from the property of the Church; and, secondly, one might consider it from its material side, and then one would define it as the right of receiving from the property of the Church an income belonging to a cleric because he holds a spiritual office established by legitimate ecclesiastical authority.

In the first definition, it is evident that the spiritual office is the chief element, and the right of receiving the income is entirely secondary and annexed to the sacred ministry. In the latter definition, the term benefice signifies the right to receive the income which is given or exists on account of an ecclesiastical office, and this primarily was the mediaeval way of looking at it, as the history of the concept will show.

No matter, then, from which viewpoint the benefice is considered, it follows that there are two chief elements constituting this ecclesiastical institute. The right of receiving

[13] Lucius Ferraris, *Prompta Bibliotheca Canonica, Iuridica, Moralis, Theologica, necnon Ascetica, Polemica, Rubricistica, Historica,* (9 vols., Romae: Ex Typographia Polyglotta, 1885-1899), s. v. *Beneficium,* art. 1, no. 6. See also D. LXXXI, 16; X, III, 5, 16.

income constitutes the formal element of a benefice, and the spiritual office is the foundation or cause of that right. This right to the income from ecclesiastical property was called a "spiritual right" or at least "annexed to the spiritual" because a benefice was given solely by reason of a sacred office. Innocent III (1198-1216) in a decretal referred to the benefice as a spiritual right.[14] Yet this right is not primarily a spiritual right, but rather a temporal one, because it is the right of receiving income which is temporal; but it is dependently connected with a spiritual thing inasmuch as it presupposes the clerical state and is given because of an ecclesiastical office. It is evident that this right is intimately connected with a spiritual thing. Thus one who attempted to purchase a benefice was guilty of simony according to a decretal of Innocent III to the Archbishop of Canterbury.[15] Pope Innocent acknowledged that clerics had the right of receiving income from ecclesiastical property: "... qui altari servit, vivere debet de altari."[16] This right, therefore, properly exists because it arises from a spiritual office and is dependent upon it. One might sum this all up with this mediaeval maxim: *beneficium datur propter officium.*[17] Needless to say, this conception was clarified only gradually, for canonical legislation and science had to overcome the more materialistic implications of the early mediaeval practice of benefices.

Historically the origins of this concept reach back into Christian antiquity. During Apostolic times as well as in the first centuries of the Church the clergy were recruited from the poorer classes and were expected for the most part to see to their own welfare. It was not too long, however, before bishops, charged as they were with the administration

[14] X, III, 5, 25 as catalogued in Augustus Potthast, *Regesta Pontificum Romanorum inde ab anno post Christum natum MCXCVIII ad annum MCCCIV*, (2 vols., Berolini, 1874-1875), no. 3989. (Hereafter cited Potthast).

[15] X, V, 3, 38; Potthast, no. 5037.

[16] X, III, 5, 16, Potthast, no. 71.

[17] I, 3, 2, in VI°.

of the temporalities of their dioceses *(paroeciae)*, found themselves obliged to assist their clergy.[18] Rather early the archpriest as well as the other members of the city-clergy were given a *stipendium* by their bishops, consisting of food and clothing, as well as other *munera*, for example, a horse. On the other hand, the rural-clergy obtained their livelihood from their rural baptismal churches. A little later the rural archpriest was given a tenure of land, called a *precarium*. This was a revocable right of tenure which the bishop gave in addition to the revenues of the baptismal church, or as a substitute for the *stipendium*.

Thus the welfare of the diocesan clergy was maintained in the ancient Church, and it remained so until the invasions of the Germanic tribes; for until the end of the Roman epoch the Canon Law had accorded to the local bishops this power of conferring all churches within their territories. With the Christianization of the Germanic peoples, however, and the ensuing infiltration of their influence over the European continent, a new order gradually evolved. This happened despite the fact that the ecclesiastical legislation on this point remained unaltered.

This policy of extreme transition in the administration of ecclesiastical appointments had its roots in the early Germanic concept of property, the *Eigenkirchenwesen*. Literally this would be translated as a system of owned churches. The more acceptable English equivalent is the system of proprietary churches.[19]

According to this early Germanic concept a church was devoid of all juridic personality. It was merely a tenement owned by the lord of the manor as a financial investment. His primary interest was profit. The essential requirement he demanded of his hired cleric was a sharp business acu-

[18] For a detailed analysis of the historical development of the concept of a benefice see G. Mollat, "Benefices Ecclésiastiques en Occident," in the *Dictionaire de Droit Canonique* (Paris: Libraire Letouzey et Ané, 1924-), Vol. III, col. 406a ff.

[19] Ulrich Stutz, *Die Eigenkirche als Element des mittelalterlich-Germanischen Kirchenrechtes*, (Berlin: H. B. Müller, 1895).

men rather than any spiritual qualifications. In fact, he tended to encourage the disobedience of the latter towards his bishop.

The origin of the ecclesiastical benefice is not then to be sought in the institutions of the Roman period of Canon Law, but rather in the institutions of Frankish law. In fact, it arose as a revolt by ecclesiastical authority against this proprietary church concept. A way had to be found to give the clergy the assurance of a livelihood, and yet maintain their freedom. The Frankish law offered an excellent means in the benefice, the only type of land tenure which did not interfere with the freedom of the tenant.

This institute of Frankish law had arisen during the troublous centuries of the Dark Age when the lot of the small proprietor had become increasingly hard. Often, to secure necessary protection or relief from oppressive exactions, he would give his land to a church and receive it back as a benefice *(beneficium)*, an estate received from the Church in return for some service, whether substantial or nominal. In like manner, Charles Martel (714-741), when needing horsemen with which to combat the Saracens and lacking the funds to hire them, offered some of his land holdings as well as some seized Church property to his own retainers as life estates, or benefices, and required in return some military service with horses and men.[20]

A benefice was the only type of tenure which did not interfere with the freedom of the tenant. The tenure of benefice, therefore, could be applied for the purpose of the tenure of a cleric, and when applied in this way it was essentially different from the purely feudal tenure, because it did not make the cleric subject to the grantor. Vassalage was not present between the priest and the manorial owner. Tenure of the estate was given to the priest without fealty or vassalage, and as such was called the *franca eleemosyna* or *Frankalmoign* given by the owner to the priest.

[20] For a historical analysis see Carl Stephenson, *Mediaeval History*, (New York: Harper & Brothers, 1935), pp. 237 ff.

The main difference between the feudal benefice and the ecclesiastical benefice was that in the latter the tenure ended with the death of the cleric, whereas the feudal benefice ended only with the death of either the lord or his vassal. Like the feudal benefice, however, the ecclesiastical benefice was bestowed through an act of investiture, a solemn surrendering of the Missal and a rod, signifying the seizin of the real estate. In return the cleric had to give the lord a remuneration for the investiture, called an *exenium* or sometimes a *conductus*.

This formality of investiture necessarily led to abuse. Many of the councils of the ninth century set about to protect the rights of the clergy. Their legislation, nevertheless, was ineffective. It is at this point in history that the great lay investiture struggle began. Through the great reform movement of Gregory VII (1073-1085), reaching its climax in the Concordat of Worms (1122), the Church was finally successful in wresting from the laity the power over benefices. Thus it was that the concept of an ecclesiastical benefice evolved.

ARTICLE II. THE CONCEPT OF ECCLESIASTICAL JURISDICTION IN THE MIDDLE AGES

The purpose and object of a society is the pursuit and attainment by its members of some common end by the use of some common means. Experience, however, has proved over and over again—so much so, indeed, that it has long been a first principle of practical life—that no society, from the sovereign State to the smallest club, is successful, unless it is governed by some competent authority. There must be some ruling power, whether individual or collective, whose office it is to govern, direct, legislate, judge, and even coerce and punish, all with the one object of securing the success of the society in the achievement of the purpose of its existence, which is the good, happiness, pleasure, in some way or other, of its members. This ruling authority or power of government is called jurisdiction.

The Church founded by Jesus Christ also needs, like every society, a regulating or authoritative power. This power Christ bestowed upon it. Directly before His Ascension He gave to the Apostles collectively the commission, and with it the authority, to proclaim His doctrine to the world at large.[21]

To enable the Church to carry out Christ's commission of leading mankind to salvation, it has been vested by Him with a threefold power, corresponding to His own office of Prophet, Priest, and King: that of teaching, its *doctrinal* authority; that of order, its *ministerial* authority; that of government, its *jurisdictional* authority. One may note in passing that some theologians make further subdivisions within these three powers and arrange them differently,[22] while others point out that they are fundamentally reducible to two, that of order and that of jurisdiction.[23]

In addition to its authority to teach men the way of salvation, the Church has also been given the effective power to guide them along its course. The right to rule, no less than the right to teach, is an integral part of its saving mission as established by its Founder.[24] The government of the Church falls under three heads: the authority which it possesses is legislative, judicial, and coercive. It should be borne in mind that this governmental authority was given directly and immediately by Christ to the Apostles and their successors, and not to the Church as a whole or to the collectivity of the faithful.[25] In other words, this power is now vested in the Supreme Pontiff, the Bishop of Rome, as well as in all of the other bishops of the world who are in communion with him. The constitution of the Church is thus

[21] Matt. 28, 18 ff.

[22] Reginald Maria Schultes, O. P., *De Ecclesia Catholica*, ed. a E. Pratner (Parisiis: P. Lethielleux, 1931), pp. 329-332.

[23] Louis Cardinal Billot, *De Ecclesia Christi* (3. ed., Prati: Giachetti, 1909), pp. 339-342.

[24] John, 20, 21; Matt., 18, 18, and 28, 19-20.

[25] Instances of the use of this power in the Apostolic Church: I Cor. 4, 21; 5, 1 ff; 6, 1 ff; II Cor. 12, 10; I Tim. 1, 20; 5, 19 ff.

hierarchic, since its pastors derive their office from a sharing of this power given by Christ. This power, then, as here described, i. e., jurisdiction strictly so called, can be defined as a power of rulership *(potestas regendi seu regiminis),* and as such is to be distinguished from the ministerial power of the Church, the power of orders. It is easy to see, then, from all that has been said, how the concepts of an ecclesiastical office and of jurisdiction have always been closely allied, and in fact often united in the one concept.

Among the Roman lawyers of old the concept of jurisdiction was not nearly as clearly defined as has been outlined above. In fact, the term *iurisdictio* itself is not found too frequently in the sources, and when it is, it specifically refers to the power and activity of *ius dicere,* that is, of establishing legal principles which serve to adjust controversies. For the Roman, then, *iurisdictio* covered any judicial activity in civil matters, and in a broader sense all activity connected with the administration of justice. With reference to the praetor, the judicial magistrate *par excellence* of classical times, it embodied all the acts and orders issued by him during the stage *in iure* of a civil trial, such as the appointment of a *iudex* (private juror), the grant of action to the plaintiff as well as its denial, the order of the judge to decide the case in dispute, and so on. Likewise, in a territorial sense, *iurisdictio* referred to the judicial district in which a magistrate could exercise his jurisdictional rights. Under the Empire, however, all higher officials were vested with *iurisdictio,* and thus the term came to have a wider extension, so much so that the entire administrative authority of the provincial governors was referred to as *iurisdictio.*[26]

[26] Dig., II, 1, 10. See also: Adolf Berger, "Encyclopedic Dictionary of Roman Law," Vol. 43, part 2, of the *Transactions of the American Philosophical Society* (Philadelphia, 1953), s. v. *iurisdictio.* This evolution of concept and metonymic use of the term *iurisdictio* is also to be found in the mediaeval canonical jurisprudence, as later chapters in this study will show. It is worth noting here, however, that the concept of *iurisdictio* in Canon Law and in the English Common

Roman Law, however, did possess a concept of jurisdictional or governing authority, although it was never consolidated into one specific legal concept. For example, it was sometimes referred to as an *auctoritas* or *potestas,* and as such either denoted the office itself, or embodied all the rights and duties connected with a particular magistracy (e. g., the *ius edicendi,* the *ius coercendi*).[27] Again, it was called *imperium* or the official administrative, legislative, and military authority possessed by the *magistratus maiores* under the Republic and the emperor under the Empire.[28] Finally, it was quite frequently referred to as *administratio*[29] or *cura,*[30] and as such embraced the totality of the governing authority possessed by public officials.

It is interesting to note that the early conciliar legislation of the Church shows a parallel development among the canonists. Such expressions as *potestas*[31] and *sub iure habere*[32] were used as synonymous with jurisdiction, and signify executive power in general, since it seems that judicial and legislative power had not as yet been crystallized in this concept.[33]

Law is identical; whereas the continental civil law still retains the classical Roman concept.

27 *Potestas:* Dig., I, 21, 5; I, 12; *auctoritas:* Justinian, Nov.,11; Gaius, Inst., IV, 46, 139.

28 Dig., LXIII, 1, 32; I, 21, 1, § 1.

29 Dig., XXVI, 7; L, 8; C., V, 37; I, 49; Just. Edict., 13, cap. 22.

30 Inst., I, 23; Dig., XXVI, 7; XVII, 5; C., V, 31-34, 36-39, 57, 60-69.

31 Canon 6 and 51 of IV Toledo (633) as found in Franciscus Gonzales, *Collectio Canonum Ecclesiae Hispanae* (Matriti: Ex Typographia Regia, 1808), col. 378 (hereafter cited Gonzales); canon 11 of I Orange, Gonzales, col. 274; canon 19 of the Synod of Arles (511), as found in Ioannes D. Mansi, *Sacrorum Conciliorum Nova et Amplissima Collectio* (53 vols. in 60, Parisiis, Arnhem, Lipsiae, 1901-1927), VIII, 345 (hereafter cited Mansi).

32 Canon 3 of the Council of Coyanza (1050). For a detailed study of this canon see: Alfonso Garcia Gallo, "El Concilio de Coyanza," *Annuario de Historia del Derecho Español,* Tom XX (1950), pp. 291 ff.

33 This does not mean to say that in the "Old Catholic" Church—as Rudolf Sohm and his colleagues contend (for example, Walter Lowrie,

These expressions are again found in the *Decretum Gratiani* (1140).[34] The term *iurisdictio* itself, on the other hand, is found in some few instances in the text of the *Decretum,* but it is used only in a rather generic and undefined fashion. In fact, there seems to have been considerable confusion among the canonists of the Middle Ages when they tried to define and limit the essential elements in the concept of jurisdiction for their own day.

Van de Kerckhove[35] admirably solves this problem through his detailed analysis of the concepts of the *lex diocesana,*[36] the *lex iurisdictionis,*[37] and the *potestas clavium* as found in the writings of the Decretists and the Decretalists. With regard to the *lex diocesana* and the *lex iurisdic-*

The Church and Its Organization in Primitive and Catholic Times [London: Longmans, Green, and Co., 1904]; Adolf Harnack, "The Constitution of the Church in the First Two Centuries," trans. by F. L. Pogson, *Modern Theological Library,* Vol XXXI [New York: G. P. Putnam's Sons, 1910] pp. 175 ff.) there was no concept of jurisdictional power, or that the power of orders and the power of jurisdiction were but one—an error which would lead to an overthrow of the divine constitution of the Church as an external society with power to legislate, as well as to a Donatistic concept of orders.

[34] *Auctoritas:* D. XLVI, 10; C. XVI, q. 1, c. 2; C. XVI, q. 7, c. 1; *potestas:* C. X, q. 1, c. 2, 3, 4, 5, 6, 7; *curam animarum habere:* C. XVI, q. 2, c. 6; *ditio:* C. XXIV, q. 1, c. 34.

[35] P. Martinien de Roulers (Van de Kerckhove), O. M. Cap., *La Notion de Juridiction dans la Doctrine des Décrétistes et des premiers Décrétalistes de Gratien (1140) a Bernard de Bottone (1250)* (Assisi: Collegio San Lorenzo da Brindisi, 1937). A summation of Van de Kerckhove's doctrine is contained in "De notione iurisdictione apud Decretistas et priores Decretalistas," *Jus Pontificium,* XVIII (1938), pp. 10-14.

[36] "... est autem lex diocesana, qua episcopus potestatem habet dispensandi spiritualia et ministros instituendi et ordinandi, quartam et cathedraticam exigendi..." Rufinus, *Summa Decretorum,* ad C. I, q. 1, c. 1, as found in *Die Summa Decretorum des Magister Rufinus,* ed. by H. Singer, (Paderborn, 1902), p. 301.

[37] "... lex iurisdictionis est qua episcopus potest clericos ordinare, altaria, ecclesia, et virgines consecrare, corrigere, suspendere, cognoscere de causis civilibus et criminalibus, et generaliter ad suam iurisdictionem pertinet omnia sacramenta conferre..." Casus, ad C. X, q. 1, c. 1.

tionis he notes a progressive development in the canonical thought between the years 1140 and 1250.

In the first period, which according to Van de Kerckhove extends from the *Decretum Gratiani* (1140) to the *Summa* of Siccard of Cremona (1180), the canonists did not use the term *iurisdictio* as such, but spoke rather of the *lex diocesana,* which might be defined as administrative power in both spiritual and temporal affairs. It should be mentioned that during this early period there was no clear distinction between this power and the power of orders.

During the second stage of development, from the *Summa* of Hugguccio (1188) up to and including the *Apparatus* (1216) of Ioannes Teutonicus, the term *iurisdictio* was used more frequently, and for the first time the merely administrative power over temporal affairs was excluded from the ambit of the concept of jurisdiction. Thus during this period the concept was limited to the notion of executive power over spiritual things, and was referred to acts dependent upon the power of orders.

In the last period, from the IV General Council of the Lateran (1215) up to the year 1250, the word *iurisdictio* itself became common among the canonists, and for the first time the power of orders was clearly distinguished from the concept of the power of jurisdiction and at the same time was differentiated from administrative duties in purely temporal matters.

Thus the mediaeval canonists' concept of *iurisdictio* evolved as that of a public power in the Church by which the collectivity of the faithful, a perfect society, is ruled and governed towards its final end by the threefold legislative, judicial, and coercive power necessary to that governance.

CHAPTER II

THE CONCEPT OF AN ECCLESIASTICAL OFFICE IN THE *DECRETUM GRATIANI* (1140)

The first source to be investigated in the effort of establishing the constitutive elements in the concept of an ecclesiastical office in the Middle Ages is naturally the *Decretum Gratiani* (1140). It was through the monumental work of the Camaldolese monk that the entire mass of ecclesiastical legislation which had been accumulated up to his day was collected and synthesized. Although Gratian's *Concordia Discordantium Canonum* was not an official collection, nevertheless it was so useful that it soon became the best known book of Canon Law and, as it were, ushered in the great epoch of canonical jurisprudence which was to follow. Since it serves as an introduction to the classical period of mediaeval canon law, it should then, likewise, serve as a starting point in the investigation of this basic institute of law. Once Gratian's concept of an office has been established, the steps in the development of canonical doctrine will be clearer, and the historical significance of this basic institute can thus be more effectively determined.

Perhaps the first essential clue to the concept of an ecclesiastical office should be established through an analysis of the use of this term in the twenty-fifth distinction of the *Decretum*. It is interesting to note here the brief introductory annotation Gratian offered to his treatise on offices:

> Breviter, quae inter ecclesiastica officia sit differentia monstravimus. Nunc a summo incipientes, et usque ad ultimum gradum descendentes, qualiter quisque eorum debeat ordinari, sanctorum auctoribus ostendamus.[1]

In the first canon of Distinction XXV one finds Gratian using as a source a letter addressed by Saint Isidore of Seville to Leofred, Bishop of Cordova in Spain, concerning

[1] Dict. pr. D. XXIII, 1.

ecclesiastical officials and their functions in the Church.[2] Actually through an analysis of this letter as well as of the famous *De ecclesiasticis officiis* of Saint Isidore one is able to arrive at the concept of an office which was prevalent in seventh-century Spain. The great bishop of Seville spoke of the offices which belong to the various participants in the power of orders. After the customary salutation to Leofred, he proceeded: "... gratias ago Deo, quod sollicitudinem officii pastoralis impendis, qualiterque ecclesiastica officia ordinentur, perquiris ...," and then listed various officials of the Church and their functions and duties, for example:

> ... Ad psalmistam pertinet officium canendi, dicere benedictiones, laudes, sacrificii responsaria, et quidquid pertinet ad canendi peritiam.
>
> ... Ad diaconum pertinet assistere sacerdotibus et ministrare in omnibus, quae agentur in sacramentis Christi ... Ad ipsum quoque pertinet officium precum, et recitatio nominum ...
>
> ... Ad episcopum pertinet basilicarum consecratio, unctio altaris et confectio chrismatis. Ipse praedicta officia distribuit et ordines ecclesiasticos ...[3]

From this, then, it seems evident that an ecclesiastical office, both for Saint Isidore and Gratian, who incorporated this text in his *Decretum,* signified the functions connected with major and minor orders, and that therefore the term *officium* was synonymous with the exercise of the sacred functions and powers inherent in ordination.

The next text which one may cite occurs a number of canons later. In this instance Gratian incorporated a section of a letter of Pope Leo the Great (401-461) to all the bishops of the provinces of Italy. Gratian was concerned at this point with the ordination of serfs who as yet had not been freed by their masters. The rubric which Gratian attached to this text serves incisively to indicate his understanding of the legislation of Leo. In the first place he stated: "Servi autem ordinari prohibentur, nisi a propriis dominis liberta-

[2] For a critical analysis of this text see *Addenda* in this chapter.
[3] D. XXV, 1.

tem legitimam consequantur," and again, "Servi ad clericatus officium non promoventur,"[4] and then he quoted a section of Leo's letter:

> Nullus episcoporum servum alterius ad clericatus officium promovere praesumat, nisi forte eorum petitio aut voluntas accesserit, qui aliquid sibi in eo vindicant potestatis . . .[5]

It should here be noted that Gratian equated the power inherent in orders, in this case a rather generic idea, *clericatus officium,* with the concept of an office.

Some few canons later Gratian took up the problem of clerics being ordained to the priesthood without first having gone through the various minor and major orders which necessarily were to precede the sacerdotal ordination. He cited the text of a letter of Pope Zosimus (417-418) to Hesichius, Bishop of Salona, in which the Pontiff stated the canonical requiremennts for ordination. The rubric to this text, worth noticing, reads: "Ad sacerdotale officium nullus, nisi per singulos gradus probatus, accedat."[6] Gratian here spoke of the *sacerdotale officium,* the office of priest, which once again shows a partial identification, at least in Gratian's mind, of the concepts of sacerdotal ordination, priestly orders, and an ecclesiastical office. An office, then, was a spiritual thing, and as such consisted in the exercise of the ministerial authority established by Christ in His Church, and thus included essentially some participation in the sacramental power of orders.

It may also be mentioned here that Gratian noted a number of impediments which prohibit a man from aspiring to

[4] D. LIV, 1 (rubric).

[5] D. LIV, 1. Jaffé, *Regesta Pontificum Romanorum ab condita Ecclesia ad annum post Christum natum MCXCVIII* (ed. 2, correctam et auctam auspiciis Gulielmi Wattenbach curaverunt F. Kaltenbrunner, P. Ewald, S. Loewenfeld, 2 vols., 1885-1888). This compilation was edited by P. Ewald for the years 590-882, and is cited JE; by F. Kaltenbrunner up to the year 590, and is cited JK; and by S Loewenfeld for the years 882-1198, and is cited JL. Cf. JE, n. 402; Mansi, V, 1226.

[6] D. LIX, 2 (rubric). JK, n. 339; Mansi, IV, 347.

sacred orders. Once again the identification of sacred orders with an ecclesiastical office should be noted:

> Ad clericatus officium non admittuntur apostatae.[7]
>
> Non admittantur curiales ad clericale officium.[8]
>
> Corpore vero vitiati similiter a sacris officiis prohibentur.[9]
>
> Presbyterorum filii ad sacra officia non sunt admittendi.[10]
>
> Filii presbyterorum ab sacris ordinibus removentur.[11]

After treating of the various grades and orders to be found in the Church, Gratian closed this section of his *Decretum* with the following telling words: "Haec de ordinandis et ordinationibus atque de singulorum graduum distinctionibus et officiis dixisse nos sufficiat."[12]

Another approach in establishing the concept of an ecclesiastical office can be made through what one may term a process of elimination. Quite frequently in the *Decretum* the two concepts of benefice and office are used in close conjunction with one another, and then at times separately as well. Perhaps then upon an analysis of the use of the two terms by Gratian one may be able to derive another definition of an office. It is also apropos at this point to recall what has been previously said concerning the mediaeval concept of an ecclesiastical benefice.

First of all, in dealing with this unified concept of office and benefice, one should remark that Gratian seemed not to make any incisive distinction between the two except in penal matters. He generally spoke only of degradation, suspension, or removal from office. It is to be noted, however, that in some few cases a cleric, when guilty of a crime, was to be suspended as well as deprived of his benefice, whereas for other crimes he was to be deprived of one or the other.

Thus Pope Alexander II (1061-1073) in a decretal to the bishops and king of Dalmatia declared that a bishop, a

[7] D. L, 69 (rubric).

[8] D. LI, 3 (rubric).

[9] D. LV, 1 (rubric).

[10] D. LVI, 1 (superscriptio).

[11] D. LVI, 1 (rubric).

[12] D. LXXXI, 1 (superscriptio).

priest, or a deacon, if he harbored a woman, was to be deprived of both his office and benefice:

> Si quis amodo episcopus, presbyter, diaconus feminam acceperit vel acceptam retinuerit, proprio gradu decidat, usque dum ad satisfactionem veniat, nec in choro psallentium maneat, nec aliquam portionem de rebus ecclesiasticis habeat.[13]

Gratian prefaced this canon with the following rubric: "Officio et beneficio privetur episcopus, presbyter, diaconus uxorem suscipiens, vel susceptam habens."[14] It should be stressed here, as in all of the examples cited in this regard, that for Gratian the *officium* appeared to connote the exercise of the functions inherent in the *sacer ordo:* ". . . nec in choro psallentium maneat." It is to be noted also that the benefice is spoken of as the ". . . portio de rebus ecclesiasticis."

Gratian then continued in the same vein in the next canon, again quoting Alexander II, who on the occasion addressed himself to the clerics of Milan:

> Si quis sacerdotum vel diaconorum vel subdiaconorum officium contumaciter deserens feminam sibi potius elegerit, sicut sponte ob fornicationem dimittit officium, ita praevaricationem dimittere cogatur etiam invitus beneficium.[15]

There were also some crimes for which a cleric was to be punished by not being permitted to exercise his office while he still retained his rights to the income from his benefice, for example: "Perpetuo careat officio presbyter, qui ira commotus, licet extra animum, aliquem interfecerit";[16] and conversely, in his treatise on simony, Gratian listed a crime

[13] D. LXXXI, 16. JL, n. 4477; Mansi, XIX, 977.

[14] D. LXXXI, 16 (rubric).

[15] D. LXXXI, 17. JL, n. 4612; Mansi, XIX, 978.

[16] D. L, 39 (rubric). The following rubrics also may be quoted as illustrating the point in question: D. XVIII, 16: "Ab officio abstineat presbyter non legalibus nuptiis detentus"; D. XLV, 7: "Deiiciatur ab officio presbyter et diaconus et episcopus verberibus timeri quaerens"; D. XLVI, 3: "Adulator vel proditor ab officio degradetur"; D. XLVI, 5: "Removeatur ab officio clericus maledicus"; D. L, 4: "Post peractum homocidium sacerdotale officium administrari non potest."

for which a cleric, while still retaining his office, was to be deprived of the fruits of his benefice.[17]

The fiftieth Distinction in the *Decretum Gratiani* is of importance in its dealing with the crimes perpetrated by clerics and with the necessary sanction which was to fall upon the delinquent. Gratian introduced his subject by noting that there are many crimes for which clerics are to be suspended from office, some of them so serious that, even after the requisite penance had been performed, the clerics must remain suspended from the exercise of their clerical functions. Throughout the sixty-nine canons of this distinction many instances are to be noted in which the terms *officium* and *sacer ordo* were used convertibly by Gratian.[18]

After this rather cursory consideration of the question, one may next seek to analyze a few of the canons which Gratian incorporated in his *Decretum* with reference to the punishment of delinquent clerics. In the first place, a text taken from the Melfi Synod of 1089, presided over by Pope Urban II (1088-1099), ought to be noted. Gratian's rubric at this point sets forth the matter in question: "Beneficio et officio careant qui post diaconatum uxoribus vacant." Thereafter follows the canon itself:

> Eos, qui post diaconatum uxoribus vacare voluerint, ab omni ordine removemus, officio atque beneficio ecclesiae carere decrevimus.[19]

At first sight the distinction made here between *ordo, officium,* and *beneficium,* seems to imply a basic difference between the concepts of *ordo* and *officium,* which in all other instances are used as convertible terms in the *Decretum.* Gratian's rubric to his particular canon, however, solves the difficulty by totally disregarding the phrase "... ab omni ordine removemus ...," which seems to imply once again

[17] C. I, q. 5, c. 1, rubric reads: "De parvulis, qui cupiditate parentum ecclesias emunt."

[18] D. L, 4, 6, 7, 19, 21, 39. The rubrics likewise serve as indications of the point alleged, e. g., c. 4: "Post peractum homocidium sacerdotale officium administrari non potest"; c. 6: "Qui se defendendo paganum occiderit, sacerdotale careat officio."

[19] D. XXXII, 10. JE, n. 5408; Mansi, XX, 725.

an identification of the two concepts, *ordo* and *officium*, which one does find throughout the *Decretum*.

The Council of Neocaesarea (314-325) had enacted a somewhat similar canon with regard to those who were in priestly orders. This canon Gratian also incorporated:

> Presbyter si uxorem duxerit, ab ordine illum deponi debere. Quodsi fornicatus fuerit, vel adulterium commiserit, extra ecclesiam abici et ad poenitentiam inter laicos redigi oportet.[20]

The glossator's (Ioannes Teutonicus, c. 1216) notation at the words *ab ordine* in this text is worthy of mention here. He noted that a priest who attempted marriage, in being deposed from his orders, was to be deprived of his office only, and not also from his benefice.

In the second part of the *Decretum* Gratian treated the question of clerics who deserted their offices. He quoted a number of canons from councils as well as papal legislation to show what penalties were to be meted out to the delinquent clerics. Among these one may cite a canon taken from the Council of Antioch, held in the year 341:

> Si quis presbyter, vel diaconus, vel quilibet clericus, deserta sua ecclesia, ad aliam transeundum esse crediderit, et ibi paullatim temptet, quo migravit, perpetuo permanere, ulterius ministrare non debet, praesertim si ab episcopo suo adrevertendum fuerit exhortatus. Quod si post evocationem sui episcopi non obedierit, sed inobediens perseveraverit, omnimodis ab officio suo deponi debere, nec aliquando spem restitutionis habere.[21]

It seems from this as well as the other legislation involved at this place in the *Decretum* that a cleric, no matter in what grade of sacred orders he was, as long as he was guilty of deserting his office, was to be removed from that office;

[20] D. XXVIII, 9, which is canon 1 of the Council, as found in Mansi, II, 540. For a comparative study of the various Latin readings of this canon, see *Ecclesiae Occidentalis Monumenta Iuris Antiquissima*, ed. by Cuthbert H. Turner (2 vols., Oxford: Clarendon Press, 1899-1939), Vol. II, Pars Prior, pp. 118 ff. (Hereafter cited Turner).

[21] C. VII, q. 1, c. 24, which is canon 3 of the Council as found in Mansi, II, 1310, and Turner, II, Pars Altera, pp. 242 ff.

in other words, he was forbidden the exercise of the sacred orders which he had received.

The concept of a sacred office included for Gratian not only the orders themselves, but the exercise of those orders, or what may be termed the liturgical functions connected with them. One finds some rather interesting texts in this regard in connection with Gratian's consideration of the problem of a minister who because of old age or for some other infirmity was unable to carry out the functions of his office. The following rubrics may be cited:

> . . . quando aliquis vel senectute vel infirmitate gravatus susceptum officium administrare non valet, si alium sibi substitui petierit, rationabiliter fieri potest.[22]
>
> Ne autem huiuscemodi passionibus sacerdotibus subito occupati coeptum officium inexpletum remaneat, institutum est, ut sacerdos, sive psallens sive sacrificans, alios secum habeat, qui si huiusmodi casus intervenerit, inchoata mysteria perficere valeant.[23]

The interesting point here is the identification of the notion of an office with its functions, showing the intimate relationship between these two factors in the one concept.

A final question to be considered if one seeks to vindicate the convertibility of the concepts of *sacer ordo* and *officium* is: was it possible for a layman to hold an ecclesiastical office? At Gratian's time the matter was quite simple, but later on the Decretists and Decretalists were to go into this problem at great length before they were able to resolve the question in their own minds.

The answer to this question can be found in the eighty-ninth Distinction, where Gratian was concerned with the functions of the *vicedominus* in the episcopal curia.[24] He began his analysis of the duties of the procurator by stating that every bishop was to have this functionary in his curia,

[22] C. VII, q. 1, c. 12 (rubric).

[23] C. VII, q. 1, c. 14 (dictum).

[24] Hereafter reference will be made to this functionary as a procurator for the lack of a better English equivalent.

and that it was the bishop's right to appoint and dismiss him. Then Gratian, in adverting to his tasks, quoted the Council of Chalcedon (451): "...placuit, omnes ecclesias habentes episcopos etiam economos habere de proprio clero, qui gubernant res ecclesiae cum arbitrio sui episcopi..."[25]

The procurator, then, was the administrator of the *res ecclesiae* in the bishop's curia, and it appears that a layman could hold this office, since no exercise of the power of orders was demanded. It is to be noted, however, from the words of the canon, that the bishop was to choose his procurator *de proprio clero*. Gratian followed this up immediately with the text of a letter of Pope Gregory I (590-604) reaffirming this precise point. His rubric succinctly sums up the point in question: "Saecularibus viris res ecclesiasticae non committantur." Then there is quoted the text of the letter itself:

> ...De cetero vero cavendum est a fraternitate vestra, ne saecularibus viris atque sub regula vestra non degentibus cuiuslibet res ecclesiae committantur, sed probatis de officio vestro clericis, in quibus, si quid reperiri poterit pravitatis, ut in subditis emendare quod illicite gestum fuerit valeatis; quo videlicet apud vos habitus sui officium magis convenienter administrent, quam accusent.[26]

It is evident from this text that this purely administrative post demanded the clerical state, in effect equating the notion of ordination and office, and implying once again the necessity of an inherent ministerial capacity in the holder of an ecclesiastical office.

In conclusion it is to be noted that there is some evidence in the *Decretum Gratiani* of the concept of a governing or jurisdictional authority in certain offices, specifically in the episcopal office. The *Magister* could well preface his remarks with this maxim: "...quando celsior gradus, tanto maior

[25] D. LXXXIX, 4, which canon 26 of the Council as found in Mansi, VII, 400.

[26] D. LXXXIX, 5. JE, n. 1731.

auctoritas invenitur."[27] In any well constituted society the incumbents in the higher offices must necessarily possess a governing authority over the ones who are subject to them. The early conciliar legislation bore this out, and it is in this context that the canonical concept of a jurisdictional authority originated.

It is worth noting that the legislation which Gratian cited in establishing these episcopal prerogatives stems almost entirely from the provincial councils held in Spain during the sixth and seventh centuries.[28] Evidently the authority of the Spanish bishops had been frequently questioned, and the fathers of these councils were very definite in the statement of their rights over the churches within the confines of their dioceses.

Gratian introduced his treatise with the following:

> Quidam laicus basilicam a se factam a diocesana lege segregare quaerit: episcopus ecclesiam cum omni dote sua ad suam dispositionem pertinere contendit . . . modo primum quaeritur, an basilica cum omni dote sua ad episcopi ordinationem pertineat?[29]

This text as well as the others cited in this *Causa* illustrate the extension of the concept for Gratian. The concept involved an administrative authority over the temporalities within a diocese. Future canonists, however, as this study will show, were to develop this concept, so that within the one hundred and fifty years after Gratian the complete canonical theory on jurisdictional power and its inherence in the concept of an ecclesiastical office was to be unfolded.

[27] D. XXI, 3 (dictum): ". . . In maioribus siquidem est regendi et iubendi potestas, in minoribus obsequendi necessitas . . ."

[28] For example: C. X, q. 1, c. 1, which is canon 15 of the Council of Lerida (546), as found in Gonzales, col. 314; c. 2, which is canon 19 of III Toledo (589), Gonzales, col. 353; c. 6, which is canon 33 of IV Toledo (633), Gonzales, col. 378.

[29] C. X, q. 1, c. 1 (superscriptio).

ADDENDA

A CRITICAL ANALYSIS OF D. XXV, 1

ARTICLE 1. PERSONAGES INVOLVED

Saint Isidore, Bishop and Doctor of the Church, was born (about 560) of a noble Roman family of Carthagena in Spain. He succeeded his elder brother, Saint Leander, as Bishop of Seville in 599 or 600. It is noteworthy that his brothers Leander and Fulgentius, and his sister Florentia, are all honored as saints. He presided over several synods and reorganized the Church of Spain, which had suffered much from Arianism. An ancient manuscript in the library of Saint Victor's Abbey in Paris has this to say: "Beatus Isidorus, Episcopus et Confessor, sive Doctor: qui regulam piissimam clericis ecclesiasticis instituit, et gentem Hispanicam suis doctrinis imbuit, totam sanctam Ecclesiam codicibus florigeris decoravit."[30]

As a writer Isidore was prolific and versatile to an extraordinary degree. It is not, however, in the capacity of an original writer, but as an indefatigable compiler of all existing knowledge, that literature is most indebted to him. His writings range over the fields of Sacred Scripture, Theology, History, and Grammar.[31] Saint Isidore died on April 6, 636, after having distributed all his earthly possessions to the poor and needy.

Leofred of Cordova, however, seems shrouded in the mists of the historical past. All that can positively be established is that he was Bishop of Cordova, a suffragan of the Metro-

[30] Quoted in *Opera Omnia Sancti Isidori,* ed. by Iacobus du Breul, (Coloniae Agrippinae, Antonius Hierat, 1617), p. ix.

[31] *Opera Omnia:* first edition was published in folio by Michael Somnius (Paris, 1580). Another edition that is quite complete is based upon the manuscripts of Gomez, with the notes of Perez and Grail (Madrid, 1599). Based largely on the Madrid edition is the one which was published by Du Breul (Paris, 1601, and Cologne, 1617). The latest and perhaps the finest edition is that of Arevalo (7 vols., Rome, 1797-1803).

politan See of Seville. Even the spelling of his name is quite indefinite.[32]

ARTICLE 2. DATE OF COMPOSITION

To establish the date of composition of Saint Isidore's letter to Leofred of Cordova, one would naturally seek some historical reference to the reign of Leofred as Bishop of Cordova. The only extant reference to this fact lies in the subscriptions to the fourth (633) and sixth (638) Councils of Toledo, as well as in the subscription to the seventh (646) Council of Toledo, made by one Valentinian, an archpriest, and proxy for Leofred at this Council. It can likewise be established that Leofred was not the Bishop of Cordova as early as 619, since at a Spanish plenary council held in that year a certain Honorius signed for the Church of Cordova. De Aldama[33] places the beginning of his reign somewhere around the year 625, because of the position in seniority of Leofred's signature in the subscriptions to the fourth Council of Toledo. Taking into consideration, then, the fact that Isidore died in 636, the date of composition of this letter should be placed somewhere between 625 and 636.

ARTICLE 3. THE TEXT OF THE LETTER

The text of the letter of Saint Isidore to Leofred of Cordova is rather elusive, and trying to track it down is a problem for the historian. Actually, its existence was first mentioned in some of the late tenth century codices.

Isidore's works were first collected by his two disciples, Saint Braulio and Ildefonsus, shortly after his death. Neither of these, however, made any mention of this letter.

[32] Gonzales, col. 393: IV Toledo: "Leudeficus Cordubensis ecclesiae episcopus subscripsi"; col. 410: VI Toledo: "Laufredus Cordubensis ecclesiae episcopus subscripsi"; col. 419: VII Toledo: "Valentinianus archipresbyter agens vicem domini mei Laudefredi Cordubensis ecclesiae episcopi, haec statuta definiens subscripsi."

[33] Jose A. de Aldama, S. J., "Indicaciones sobre la cronologia de las obras de S. Isidoro," *Miscellanea Isidoriana* (Romae: Typis Pontificiae Universitatis Gregorianae, 1936), p. 59.

Actually it does not make its appearance in any of the collected works of Isidore until the Paris edition of Du Breul in 1601, where it is placed immediately after the *De ecclesiasticis officiis.*

One finds the letter, however, in some of the manuscript codices of the tenth and eleventh centuries. Arevalo (1747-1824), the great Isidorian scholar, tells us that it can be found in the *Codex Regio-Vaticanus 1026,* a collection of canons that are inscribed *Polycarpus,*[34] although it appears there in an abbreviated form.[35] He also cites Garcia Loaisa († 1575) who printed the letter as an appendix to his notes on the eighth Council of Toledo, where he stated that the letter was to be found in the Escorial codex, entitled *Vigilianus,* of 976.[36] This is also known as the *Codex Alveldensis,*[37] so called after the monastery where it was to be found. The text quoted by Loaisa is much longer than that in Gratian, and is what one might call a complete text of the letter. Berardi[38] also quoted this text, and on the faith of Loaisa's statement believed it to be taken from the *Codex Vigilianus.*

This seems historically inaccurate in view of the modern scholarly research which has been done on the Latin codices

[34] A canonical collection (1104-1106) made by a certain Cardinal Gregory, Bishop of Compostella, during the reign of Paschal II (1099-1118). Sources: *Decretum* of Burchard, the *Collectio Anselmi Lucensis,* the *Collectio 74 Titulorum,* and other Italian collections.

[35] Arevalo, *Isidoriana,* II, 73, as found in J. P. Migne, *Patrologiae Cursus Completus, Series Latina* (221 vols., Parisiis, 1844-1864), LXXXI, pp. 493-495 (hereafter cited *MPL*)

[36] "Ex codice MSS bibliothecae divi Laurentii perantiquo, dicto Vigiliano, excerpsi."—Reproduced in Phillipus Labbaeus, S. J., and Gabriel Cossartius, S. J., *Sacrosancta Concilia* (15 vols., Lutetiae Parisiorum, 1572), Vol. VI, col. 420.

[37] A detailed description of the contents of this codex can be found in Gonzales, folio b and c. Gonzales states at this place: "... Alveldense illud dictum est ab Alveldae monasterio non procul Lucronio, provinciae Ruconiae sive Rigoviae civitate notissima. Vigilianus autem, quoniam a monacho quodam Vigilio nomine fuerit conscriptum, appellari consuevit. . . ."

[38] Carolus Berardi, *Gratiani Canones* (5 vols., Venetiis: Ex Typographia Petri Valvensis, 1777), Vol. IV, p. 394.

in the Escorial collection, and which show that Isidore's letter to Leofred is not to be found among the documents in the *Codex Alveldensis* (d I 2).[39] The *Vigilianus* merely contains the *Collectio Hispana* as well as excerpts from the Fathers and early ecclesiastical writers. The only texts attributable to Saint Isidore in this codex are his *Contra Iudaeos* and an *Epitome librorum Divi Isidori*.

There is nevertheless in the Escorial a collection of the same period as the *Codex Alveldensis* which does contain the text of the letter. It is the *Codex Aemilianensis* (d I 1), which is dated 994.[40] On folio 336 there appears the following: "Incipit epistola beati Ysidori ivnioris eclesie ad Levdefredum episcopvm cordvbensis eclesie. Domino meo serbo Levdefredo episcopo Ysidorus. 'Perlectis sanctitatis tue litteris . . . per te remissionem consequar peccatorum. Amen.' " This then seems to have been Garcia Loaisa's source, since it printed the letter in the text which he used. The only other Escorial manuscripts which reproduce the letter are a part of a sixteenth century collection of the writings of the Fathers.[41] To try to explain this error is rather difficult, unless one assumes that, since the two manuscripts are very similar, and in fact are members of the same family, Loaisa could have mistaken the one for the other.

The first appearance of the text of the letter in any formal canonical collections is to be linked with the eleventh and twelfth centuries. These were systematic in character and formed one of the principal sources from which Gratian derived his material for the *Decretum*.

The letter appears in the *Decretorum Libri XX* of Burchard of Worms, compiled around 1022.[42] It occurs in the third book, the fiftieth chapter, under the title: *De ordinibus*

[39] P. Antolin, O.S.A., *Catalago de los Codices Latinos de la Escorial* (4 vols., Madrid: Imprinta Helenica, 1910), Vol. 1, p. 268.

[40] Gonzales, p. viii, tells us that it is called *Aemilianensis* ". . . quia in S. Aemilianensi de la Cogolla monasterio aliquot ante saeculis fuit custoditus."

[41] (b III 14).

[42] *MPL*, CXL, pp. 682 ff.

sacris. The letter in this context is abbreviated. Burchard mentioned only ten of the ecclesiastical offices, omitting the chapters on the *Archipresbyter,*[43] *Primicerius,* and *Thesaurarius.* He likewise placed in juxtaposition the various offices which he considered. In fact, his text of the letter is unique in its form.

The letter also appears in the *Decretum* (circa 1094)[44] and the *Panormia* (circa 1095)[45] of Ivo of Chartres († 1117). The text as it is reproduced in the *Decretum* is identical with the text used by Gratian. Ivo even includes the spurious chapter on the Archpriest. But in his *Panormia,* although he essentially reproduces the same text, he omits this doubtful chapter altogether. This seems to indicate Gratian's dependence upon Ivo's *Decretum* as his source for Isidore's letter to Leofred of Cordova .

Article 4. Authenticity of the Letter

The authenticity of this letter has always been a problem for Isidorian scholars. Some have questioned it in its entirety, while others have only doubted that certain sections came from the pen of the *Doctor Egregius.* The *Correctores Romani* noted that the section on the Archpriest was not to be found in the letter itself.[46] Arevalo is one of the few who held that it is not a spurious document.

Many theories challenge the authentic character of this letter. The letter is regarded by some as simply a reworking of Isidore's *De ecclesiasticis officiis.* Although these two

[43] Most authorities doubt the authenticity of this particular canon, although it is found in some texts of the letter, e. g., Ivo of Chartres, *Decretum,* as well as in the *Decretum Gratiani* (D. XXV, 1). Moreover, this identical chapter is extant in two other sources under the rubric: *Ex Concilio Toletano: Compilatio Prima,* I, 16, 1, and X, I, 24, 1. This canon is not to be found in any council of Toledo, which absence shows its spurious character.

[44] *MPL,* CLXI, pp. 447 ff.

[45] *MPL,* CLXI, pp. 1138 ff.

[46] Correctores Romani ad *Decretum Gratiani,* ad D. XXV, 1, s. v. *archiepresbyter.*

texts have certain things in common, great divergencies appear upon a comparative study of these two texts. For example, both treat in a somewhat similar fashion the offices of porter, exorcist, lector, subdeacon, and deacon. In the *De officiis,* however, there is an extensive treatment of the *tonsurati* and of the *corepiscopi,* which is peculiar to this treatise. There no mention of the *corepiscopi* in the letter to Leofred, but in its stead one does find a rather lengthy treatise on two other offices, namely, those of the Archdeacon and the *Primicerius.*

Silva-Tarouca,[47] perhaps following Berardi,[48] maintains that in this letter the office of the *corepiscopi* was purposely replaced with that of the Archdeacon. In fact, he attributes the letter to the Pseudo-Isidorians rather than to Saint Isidore, because he sees in the Archdeacon of the letter to Leofred a greater similarity to the *Archidiacones-presbyteri* of the famous *Capitula* of Hincmar of Rheims.[49] "Con Hincmaro e Leudefredo siamo in pieno ambiente Pseudo-Isidoriano. La 'bête noire' de Pseudo-Isidoro e certamente il *Chorepiscopus,* che cerca di eliminare ad ogni costo. Per sostituirvi l'arcidiacono credo che fosse fabbricata la lettera a Leudefredo."[50]

It appears apropos to interject at this point that the offices of Archpriest and Archdeacon were not unknown in the immediate post-Isidorian era in Spain. Among the canonical acts of the Council of Merida in 666 occurs the following canon:

> Communi deliberatione sancimus, ut omnes nos episcopi infra nostram provinciam constituti in cathedralibus nostris ecclesiis singuli nostrum archipresbyterum, archidiaconum, et primicerium habere decrevimus; sanctus quippe est ordo et a nobis per omnia observandus.[51]

47 Carlo Silva-Tarouca, S. J., "Nuovi studi sulle antiche lettere dei Papi," *Gregorianum,* XII (1931) pp. 581 ff.

48 Berardi, *op cit.,* Vol. IV, col. 393.

49 *MPL,* Vol. CXXV, col. 802.

50 Silva-Tarouca, "art. cit.", p. 582.

51 Canon 60 of the Council of Merida as found in Hermann T.

Berardi also considered the letter to be spurious. His primary reason for doubting that Isidore wrote it was the difference between the matters treated in the letter and in the *De ecclesiasticis officiis,* and he added that the textual differences of the letter itself in the various codices, where it appears in greater length in some than in others, seem to challenge its authentic character.

Sejourné[52] is one modern author who seems to feel that this letter really came from the pen of Saint Isidore, but he appears to contradict himself. In the early section of his book he defends the authenticity of the text,[53] whereas later on[54] he regards the letter as a document of the middle of the seventh century, but definitely still of Visigothic origin. About all that one can say at this point is: *adhuc sub iudice lis est.*

Bruns, *Canones Apostolorum et Conciliorum Veterum Saeculorum IV-VII* (2 vols., Berlin: G. Remerius, 1839), Vol. I, p. 47.

[52] P. Sejourné, *Saint Isidore de Séville: sons rôle dans l'histoire du droit canonique* (Paris: Gabriel Beauchesne, 1929).

[53] *Ibid.,* p. 39.

[54] *Ibid.,* p. 166.

CHAPTER III

THE CONCEPT OF AN ECCLESIASTICAL OFFICE IN THE PRINTED COMMENTARIES OF THE DECRETISTS

The previous chapter sought to determine the meaning of the concept of an ecclesiastical office as the term was used in the texts of the *Decretum Gratiani.* It reached the conclusion that to Gratian anyone participating in any degree in the ministerial power of orders could be said to have an *officium*. Needless to say, this conception, which at the same time is both too generic and also too limited, can hardly be called satisfactory, simply because the intrinsic element of jurisdictional authority and power is absent. This discrepancy, however, is understandable if one considers, first of all, the text that Gratian chose for his treatise on ecclesiastical offices. The letter of Saint Isidore of Seville to Leofred of Cordova was after all a distinctly liturgical text. Gratian in using this letter was perpetuating the ancients' concept of the *divina officia:* that is, the sacred functions proper to the participants in the sacrament of orders. Secondly, it must be borne in mind that the concept of jurisdiction itself, as Van de Kerckhove's study bears out, was not too precisely defined at that point in canonical history.

In the hundred years after Gratian the doctrine on jurisdiction was to be completely unfolded by the canonists, and along with this genesis came a parallel development in the canonical doctrine on ecclesiastical offices. This growth was due to the monumental task accomplished by the Bolognese Master, the Father of the Science of Canon Law. For with the appearance of his *Decretum* the canonists' activity changed its shape from that of a more or less imperfect collecting of manifold sources into that of a scientific reasoning on and interpreting of the sources. Canon Law became a system of concepts and rules, a juridical self-supporting science by the writing and teaching of this eminent man. Upon the foundation he laid, a school of Canon

Law arose for the first time in the history of the Church. His *Decretum* was publicly taught and lectured upon, first by the *Magister* himself, and later by his pupils and disciples. These lectures gave rise to a vast literature in ecclesiastical jurisprudence. In the present chapter a study of a few of the commentaries of these early Decretists is presented with the hope that the jurisprudence of these canonists will help to elucidate the development in the concept of an ecclesiastical office. This study, however, has necessarily been limited to the printed sources because of the inaccessibility of manuscripts. The writer fully realizes that a wealth of this material still remains only in manuscript, yet it was felt that an adequate statement of the Decretists' jurisprudence could be established from the printed sources.

Article 1. The Concept of Sacred Orders

Since Gratian seemed to equate the term *officium* with the ministerial powers inherent in sacred ordination, it would be appropriate to present first a little of the detailed analysis of the concept of orders as it is found in the commentaries of the Decretists.

> In ecclesiasticis officiis adipiscendis duo maxime attenduntur, electio, scilicet et ordinatio. Et quidem electio prior est tempore, sed ordinatio anterior dignitate.[1]

Sacred ordination is indeed an intrinsic element in the concept of an office, and therefore the doctrine on this institute is pertinent to our study.

Paucapalea, Gratian's earliest commentator, followed the teaching of his master. He, too, did not separate the functions of the *sacer ordo* and *officium*. For example:

> Monachi sacerdotes, si a populo fuerint electi et ab episcopo cum consensu abbatis ordinati ac in parochialibus ecclesiis instituti, omnia officia sacerdotalia administrare licite valent, i. e., habent pot-

[1] *Die Summa Decretorum des Magister Rufinus*, ed. by Heinrich Singer (Paderborn: Verlag von Ferdinand Schöningh, 1902), ad D. LX, in principio, s. v. *ecce ex parte*, p. 151. (Hereafter cited Rufinus, *Summa*).

> estatem praedicandi, baptizandi, poenitentiam dandi, peccata remittendi.[2]

The Decretists, however, were confronted with the problem as to which "offices" or grades of orders were to be considered as necessary parts of the sacrament. Relying on Saint Isidore, many felt that all officials in the Church participated in sacred orders, but as the anonymous author of the *Summa Parisiensis*[3] so wisely remarked: "Isidorus . . . potius intendit vocabula exponere quam ordines assignare." By way of illustration he cited the example of the *psalmistae:* ". . . qui non ordines, sed tantum habent coronam quam solebant primo facere quondam sacerdotes, sed hodie nonnisi episcopi."[4] In this connection Rufinus maintained that there were only seven "orders," as sealed in the ostiary, the exorcist, the lector, the acolyte, the subdeacon, the deacon, and the priest.[5]

Although it had always been held that the diaconate and the priesthood essentially participated in the sacramental character of orders, this was not so with reference to subdeaconship. Rufinus attempted a solution of this problem with the following distinction:

> Sacer ordo duobus modis dicitur: sive quia sacro deputatur officio, scil. altaris ministerio; sive quia

[2] *Die Summa des Paucapalea uber das Decretum Gratiani,* ed. by J. Friedrich von Schulte (Giessen: Verlag von Emil Roth, 1890), ad C. XVII, in principio, p. 90 (hereafter cited Paucapalea, *Summa*). Paucapalea's treatment of deposition likewise testifies to this fact: "Sacerdotes autem et levitae, si incontinentes inventi fuerint, omni officio ecclesiastico debent privari. Si autem condignam poenitentiam egerint, ea peracta in proprio ordine poterunt reparari."—*Summa,* ad D. LXXXII, p. 44.

[3] This *Summa* of an anonymous twelfth century canonist has been recently edited by Terrence P. McLaughlin, C.S.B. (Toronto: The Pontifical Institute of Mediaeval Studies, 1952). The editor proposes as an approximate date of composition the year 1160 (p. xxxii). For further details concerning this *Summa* see McLaughlin's comments in his introductory notes. (Hereafter cited *Summa Paris.*)

[4] *Summa Paris.,* ad D. XXI, 1 (McLaughlin, p. 21).

[5] Rufinus, *Summa,* ad D. LII, in principio, s. v. *qui vero* (Singer, p. 135).

> ex impositione manus episcopi et consecratione traditur.[6]

He then explained his distinction. According to the first mode of speaking there are really three essentially constituted orders, since the subdeacon does participate in the ministry of the altar; whereas in the second instance there are only two, since in ordination to subdeaconship there is neither an imposition of hands nor a consecration with oil.

As with subdeaconship, so, too, the Decretists were not definite about episcopal orders. It was conjectured by some that the episcopacy was a dignity rather than an order. "Episcopus potius dignitatis quam ordinis est."[7]

Another interesting detail concerning the concept of orders evolved through the discussion of whether a monk was capable of holding an ecclesiastical office. The mediaeval canonist distinguished the offices of monk and cleric, and it was for the latter of these to administer the sacraments of Penance and Baptism, and to celebrate the Holy Sacrifice,[8] whereas the former in his capacity as a monk was not permitted to perform these *divina officia*. This, however, was the discipline of the primitive Church, when most monks were either anchorites or cenobites and not ordained clerics, "... quia tunc fere omnes monachi laici erant." In so far then as a monk participated in holy orders, it could be said that he possessed an ecclesiastical office and thus was able to perform the functions of that office, among which was preaching: "... nec monachus nec laicus quantumvis sapiens praedicare debet nisi sit sacerdos. Monachus vero, si est sacerdos, hoc facere potest."[9] This gloss, then, definitely

[6] Rufinus, *Summa*, ad D. XXXII, 11, s. v. *erubescant* (Singer, p. 75).

[7] *Summa Paris.*, ad D. XXI, 1; et ad D. XXXII, 1 (McLaughin, p. 31): "Hoc falsum videtur cum quatuor non sunt ordines, sed episcopatum appellat ordinem improprie pro dignitate, ut sic dignitatem accipiat pro ordine."

[8] *Summa Paris.*, ad C. XXVII, q. 1 (McLaughlin, p. 188); et ad C. XVI, q. 1, s. v. *quod monachi* (McLaughlin, p. 177): "... Nullus ergo monachus in eo quod est monachus potest celebrare officia populo quod clericorum est."

[9] *Summa Paris.*, ad C. XVI, q. 1, c. 19 (McLaughlin, p. 178).

shows that the ecclesiastical office held by an ordained priest participated in the doctrinal ministry of the Church as well as in its ministerial authority.

One of the longest and most interesting treatises to be found in the *Summa Parisiensis* is devoted to the crime of simony.[10] The author prefaced his remarks with a lengthy inquiry into those elements which constitute matters as essentially spiritual, and therefore, if these were bought or sold, would involve the sin of simony.

It was one of his great difficulties to resolve the problem concerning the validity of a simoniacal ordination, for, as he remarked, one so ordained has received a *"caput vulneratum."* Did this necessarily imply that the simonist's ordination was invalid? To solve this difficulty he instituted an important distinction with regard to sacred ordination:

> In ordinatione quatuor considerantur: sacramentum, scilicet unctio et benedictio, quae fiunt circa ordinandum; secundum potestas; tertium exsecutio, quae scilicet agit ordinatus quorum potestatem accipit; quartum scilicet ipsa spiritualis gratia, scilicet appositio virtutum et similium gratiarum.[11]

Thus a simonist's ordination was null only with regard to the functions inherent in his orders; in other words, because of his crime he was prohibited the exercise *(exsecutio)* of those orders. Further on, the *Summa Parisiensis* definitely identified this *exsecutio* of the powers received in ordination with an ecclesiastical office, maintaining that it is something intrinsically spiritual and that thus the buying and selling of it necessarily constitutes the sin of simony.

One important detail remains to be considered here concerning prelatial dignities and the rights of precedence among the participants in sacred orders.

> Praelatura in clericis provenit aliquando ex dignitate consecrationis, aliquando ex dignitate ordinis, aliquando ex dignitate administrationis.[12]

[10] *Summa Paris.*, ad C. I, q. 1, s. v. *quod autem spiritualia* (McLaughlin, p. 79).

[11] *Ibidem*, s. v. *gratia* (McLaughlin, p. 80).

[12] Rufinus, *Summa*, ad D. XXI, 2, s. v. *in novo* (Singer, p. 45).

Thus a bishop precedes all others by reason of his consecration, a deacon precedes a subdeacon because of the dignity of his orders, and, finally, an archdeacon precedes all others, even an archpriest, on account of his administrative office, even though in his orders he is necessarily lower in rank than an archpriest.

Article 2. The Concepts of Benefice and Office

As was previously mentioned, the institute of benefice was intrinsically linked to an ecclesiastical office in the doctrine of the mediaeval canonists. The lawyers had determined that the right of receiving a sustenance constituted the formal element in the institute of benefice, while the sacred office was in itself the foundation and cause of that right. This right was considered not something spiritual, but something temporal, since it consisted in the receiving of something temporal, but it was so dependently and intrinsically connected with a sacred office that one who purchased or sold a benefice was necessarily guily of simony. This doctrine was first expounded by Rufinus in the following manner:

> . . . an praebendas emere sit symoniacum. Quod ex eo probatur, quia sacris officiis ecclesiae adiunctae sunt: unde, si quis praebendas emerit, et sacra officia eo ipso videtur emisse.[13]

In this regard, however, Rufinus made a further essential distinction in the institute of benefice:

> . . . Sed attendendum est quod in ecclesiasticis beneficiis duo sunt: scilicet, ius ipsum beneficiorum, et fructus ex beneficiis percepti vel percipiendi.[14]

He further insisted that this right (*ius praebendarum*) is intrinsically linked to an office, so much so that ". . . sine eo non habetur." Accordingly a lay person, having no ministerial authority or power, could neither participate in nor possess this right. Likewise, if a delinquent cleric was de-

[13] Rufinus, *Summa,* ad C. I, q. 3, s. v. *multorum* (Singer, p. 226).
[14] *Loc. cit.*

prived of his office, it was implied that he was deprived as well of his benefice.[15]

On the other hand, the income itself (*fructus percepti vel percipiendi*) was an adjunct, and so it was not intrinsic to an office. Therefore it could be bought and sold without any implication of simoniacal intent.

Another problem in the beneficiary system of the Church which perplexed Rufinus was that of absolute ordination. Gratian had incorporated in his *Decretum* the sixth canon of the Council of Chalcedon (451).[16] This canon forbade ordination without title, that is, something which guarantees a cleric an honorable sustenance. In the early Church and for a long time after this council, the law prohibited the ordination of anyone even to minor orders who had not some definite ecclesiastical charge in a church assuring him of a respectable living. The church for which he was ordained was called the *titulus ordinationis,* and the candidate himself was said to be *intitulatus.*

The only title recognized by the Council of Chalcedon in its canon 6 was the one which later was known as the *titulus beneficii,* which connoted the cleric's assignment to a church

[15] As proof of his contention Rufinus cited the following canons: D. XXVIII, 3; D. LXXXI, 16, 17, 18; D. XCI, 3.

[16] D. LXX, 1. "Nullum absolute ordinare nec Diaconum, nec Presbyterum, nec omnino aliquem eorum, qui sunt in ecclesiastica ordinatione, nisi specialiter in Ecclesia civitatis, vel in possessione, vel in Martyrio, vel Monasterio ordinandus praedicetur: et eos vero, qui absolute ordinantur, definit sancta Synodus irritam habere huiusmodi ordinationem, et in actu invalidam, ad iniuriam ordinantis." Mansi, VI, 1226. There are many other readings of this canon in which "*praedicetur*" is rendered "*designetur*" or "*pronuntietur,*" which, according to some, would make the canon refer to the public announcement of the ordination in the Church (Mansi, VII, 362, 375), and, in fact, the version of it in the *Decretum Gratiani* unmistakably presents that meaning. However, the phrase "*absolute ordinantur*" which had a very definite meaning, namely, to be ordained without a title, i.e., without a place of employment and sustenance, is the key to the correct interpretation, and, indeed, the Fathers of the Council of Trent understood the canon in the sense of clerical assignment (sess. XXIII, *de ref.*, c. 16).

in a city, or to one in a village, or to a martyry, or to a monastery. The council had declared that absolute ordinations, that is *sine titulo,* were invalid (*irrita*). In view of the prevalence of absolute ordination in his day, Rufinus set about to explain the correct sense of the word *irrita* in the text of the canon.[17]

> Ordinatio habetur irrita tribus modis: primo, quoad sacramenti veritatem, illa est quae fit praeter formam ecclesiae vel a non habentibus potestatem; secundo, quantum ad officii executionem, ut illa, quae non fit a suo episcopo, e.g., D. LXXI, 1, et C. IX, q. 2; tertio, quoad beneficii perceptionem, ut absoluta, i. e., sine titulo facta ordinatio, ut hic dicetur: qui enim nulli ecclesiae intitulantur, a nulla ecclesia ex debito aluntur.[18]

Rufinus, however, did not seem satisfied with this distinction: "... nobis autem videtur quod duobus modis ordinatio sit dicenda vacua." To prove his contention he cited the case of the delinquent cleric (*sua culpa*) who in being deprived of his office was likewise understood to be deprived of the fruits of his benefice,[19] and vice versa;[20] and so he argued: "... si enim non est dignus minori, quomodo iudicabitur dignus maiori?" Therefore the true significance of the term *irrita* in the conciliar canon was this: when a candidate was ordained without title he was to be deprived of the functions of his office or orders as well as the fruits of any benefice he held.

ARTICLE 3. THE CONCEPTS OF OFFICE AND JURISDICTION

One finds in the commentaries of the Decretists many details that outline and distinguish the concept of the governing authority from that of the ministerial powers pos-

[17] Rufinus, *Summa,* ad D. LXX, in principio, s. v. *ab episcopis* (Singer, p. 162): "Nunc tractatum istum adaugens ostendit quod nullus clericus absque propriae ecclesiae titulo est ordinandus; alioquin irrita habetu. Ideo autem haec absoluta ordinatio prohibita est, ne vagos, seculares et acephalos redderet clericos."

[18] *Loc. cit.*

[19] C. XII, q. 2, c. 45.

[20] D. L, 39.

sessed by the Church's officials. It is to be noted that it was the analysis of the episcopal office that brought about this development of doctrine with the consequent introduction of an inherent jurisdictional capacity into the concept of that ecclesiastical office. Needless to say, it was not always called jurisdiction: it was referred to rather as a *ius,* a *potestas,* an *auctoritas,* and often a *lex.*[21] This article, then, will set forth this doctrine in a chronological study in order to enable the reader the better to appreciate this jurisprudential development.

Section 1. The "Summa" of Paucapalea (1148)

The inherence of jurisdictional powers in the concept of an office was surely not stressed in detail by Paucapalea. The writer has found only two instances in the text, thus far edited, wherein one would be at all justified in seeing any specific office invested with a capacity or a power rather than a simple ministry. The first deals with the case of a priest who in reconciling a dying excommunicated priest was said to have usurped episcopal power through his act. The reader will readily infer from this that the absolution and reconcilation of such a delinquent were reserved to episcopal authority, and therefore not inherent in the sacerdotal "office."[22] Since the *potestas ligandi et solvendi* comes

[21] The use of the word *lex* in this concept was not an innovation; rather, it originated in the jurisprudence of Rome. For example, the Romans spoke of the *lex de imperio,* which was a governing authority bestowed upon a newly elected official by the *comitia curiata,* an institute of the early imperial period. (Hans J. Wolff, Roman Law [Norman: The University of Oklahoma Press, 1951], pp. 28, 39). Likewise, in their treatment of real securities, the Romans spoke of the *lex commissoria,* which was a special clause inserted in a *pactum fiduciae* on the strength of which a creditor became the absolute owner of a mortgaged object since the debtor forfeited his rights to it through his failure to pay the debt. (Fritz Schultz, *Classical Roman Law* [Oxford: Clarendon Press, 1951], p. 414). Here again *lex* implied an authority or a power rather than in accord with its later common usage, a rule or regulation: Gaius I, 3: "Lex est quod populus iubet atque constituit."

[22] Paucapalea, *Summa,* ad C. XXVI (Schultc, p. 107): "...Ne

to a priest from the hands of a bishop, and not vice versa, therefore, so our author argued one who was condemned by a superior cannot validly be absolved by an inferior. What in reality obtained, however, was the limiting of a power in a particular office, rather than any inherence of power or authority in that office. Nevertheless, Paucapalea saw in this episcopal right (*pontificalia*) something distinct from the *ordo sacer* of the episcopacy, and thus acknowledged for the episcopal office an exclusive authority in penal matters.

The only other instance is concerned with the right of appeal and the obligation of obedience within the various hierarchical offices of the Church.

> Primates et patriarchae diversorum sunt nominum, sed eiusdem officii. Quoties necesse fuerit, episcopi ad primates ab archiepiscopis appellant, sed a primatibus ad archiepiscopos appellare non licet. Debent ergo obedientiam primatibus archiepiscopi in omnibus, quae sibi ab eis iuste fuerint imperata.[23]

This is certainly a rather subtle concept of a type of jurisdictional authority, but the question dealt indeed with an *officium* connected not in any way with a specific grade of orders, but rather with a hierarchical jurisdiction.

Section 2. The "Summa Parisiensis" (1157)

A development in the doctrine on ecclesiastical offices is also to be found in the *Summa Parisiensis*. The beginnings of an acknowledged inherent jurisdictional capacity are to be noted in several instances. For example, it was stated: "... quod episcopus debet habere ius suum in suo episco-

episcoporum officia, quorum potestas quantum ad sacerdotalem attinet dignitatem, cum presbyterio est communis, ipsi presbyteri impune usurparent, casum subnectit cuiusdam sacerdotis, qui alium sacerdotem ab episcopo notatum eodem inconsulto in extremis reconciliavit, et in hoc pontificalia usurpare non timuit ..." *Summa Paris.*, ad C. XXVI, q. 6, in principio (McLaughlin, p. 233): "... Potestas autem reconciliandi episcopalis est officii, non sacerdotalis ..."

[23] Paucapalea, *Summa*, ad D. XCIX (Schulte, p. 49).

patu."[24] This *"ius"* of the bishop is certainly not to be considered an inherent part of his episcopal orders; rather, it was an added factor, implying a right of ownership and administration over those churches that are within the confines of his diocese.

The jurisprudence of the *Summa Parisiensis* also witnesses this genesis of concept in its treatment of the penalty of excommunication.

> ... Reconciliatio publica quando publici poenitentes publice ante fores ecclesiae per manus episcopalis impositionem reconciliantur. Ista episcopis conceditur, presbyteris prohibita ...[25]

It is evident then that something more than the inherent "power of the keys" was involved in this instance. The harm done by a public sinner involved the common good of the faithful as a whole, and therefore his reintroduction into the society of the faithful demanded a public reconciliation, which was reserved to a higher authority than that possessed by a priest. This exercise of power in the external forum was certainly not intrinsic to the concept of episcopal orders; thus there was introduced a development in the concept of the ecclesiastical office of a bishop, for this power in its exercise was differentiated from the ministerial powers of the Church. It was rather in virtue of his jurisdictional authority that a bishop was concerned with the common weal of the faithful entrusted to his care, as was instanced in this case.

Section 3. The "Summa" of Rufinus (1157-1159)

The next commentary under consideration is that of Rufinus. To the casual reader this *Summa* seems much more detailed than any other thus far considered. It is not this detail, however, which is so astonishing, but rather the wealth of canonical science that is to be found in it.

[24] *Summa Paris.*, ad C. X. in principio, s. v. *laicus quidam* (McLaughlin, p. 142).

[25] *Summa Paris.*, ad C. XXVI, q. 6, in principio, (McLaughlin, p. 233).

Rufinus prefaced his remarks by stating that a bishop has the *potestas gubernandi et disponendi* regarding all things ecclesiastical within his diocese.[26] In fact, this author notes that, etymologically considered, the term *diocese* itself really implied authoritative governance.[27]

In the episcopal office Rufinus distinguished between a candidate's election to the episcopate and his subsequent ordination or consecration, whereby he became fully invested with the episcopal authority and prerogatives. This author delineated his doctrine in this regard when he attempted to solve this query: can a bishop although validly elected but not as yet consecrated, depose a cleric? Rufinus distinguished the authoritative powers inherent in the episcopal office:

> Animadvertendum est quod aliud est ius auctoritatis, aliud ius administrationis. Et quidem ius auctoritatis quemadmodum in episcopo, ad cuius ius omnes res ecclesiasticae spectare videntur, quia eius auctoritate omnia disponuntur; ius autem administrationis sicut in economo, iste habet ius administrandi, sed auctoritate caret imperandi: quicquid aliis precipit, non sua, sed episcopali auctoritate indicit.[28]

From this definition it can be inferred that the episcopal authority was quite extensive. This was true, provided the candidate had been consecrated, and therefore possessed the fullness of episcopal orders.[29] With this in mind, then, Rufinus solved his query thus:

[26] *Summa,* ad C. XI, in principio, s. v. *clericus quidam* (Singer, p. 306).

[27] Rufinus, *Summa,* ad D. XVIII, 17, s. v. *decernim* (Singer, p. 40): "Diocesis grece; latine sonat gubernatio, episcopalis, scil., ad exemplum nimirum familiae: quae gubernatur ab uno rectore, sicut diocesis ab uno pastore."

[28] Rufinus, *Summa,* ad D. XXII, 1, s. v. *omnes ... primatus* (Singer, p. 47).

[29] Rufinus, *Summa,* ad D. LX, in principio, s. v. *ecce ex parte* (Singer, p. 152): "... Cum autem quis in episcopum eligitur, non continuo plenam potestatem adipiscitur, sed usque in consecrationem differtur ..."

> Ante episcopalem unctionem ... dicimus quod plenam potestatem habeat quoad administrationem, non autem quoad auctoritatem, et ideo iure plene administrationis potest aliquos ab administratione procurationum vel ordinum suspendere ... Deponere autem, i. e., exauctorare non potest, qui plenitudinem auctoritatis nondum habet, quam ex sola consecratione est certissimum evenire.[30]

It is to be noted, then, that the authority inherent in the episcopal office was dependent in part at least upon episcopal consecration, and existed only where this was present. The evolving doctrine was to go contrary to this theory in the ensuing years.[31] This is quite easily understood when one recalls that the future canonists were clearly to distinguish between orders and jurisdiction. One cannot hope to find an incisive distinction between these two concepts in this early period, nor, in fact, any really definitive concept of jurisdiction itself. Rufinus attempted a definition of this institute in what he called the *lex dioecesana*:

> ... est autem lex dioecesana, qua episcopus potestatem habet dispensandi spiritualia et ministros instituendi et ordinandi, et visitandi et quartam exigendi in sua parochia catedraticam ...[32]

This was certainly a rather generic concept, since it included both the jurisdictional and the ministerial powers in the Church, but it must be admitted that in itself it was an advance in doctrine from that which is found in the text of the *Decretum*, since it marks the first scientific attempt to establish the juridical concept of jurisdictional power.

[30] Rufinus, *Summa*, ad D. XXIII, 1, s. v. *tamen* (Singer, p. 52).

[31] In this regard see: X, I, 6, 15, as well as the *glossa ordinaria* at this place which stated: "... Electus, confirmatus, non consecratus potest exercere quae sunt iurisdictionis, non autem ea quae sunt ordinis episcopalis."

[32] Rufinus, *Summa*, ad C. I, q. 1, c. 1, s. v. *si ex laicis* (Singer, p. 301). The term *lex dioecesana* as first used by the fathers of the Council of Lerida (546) in Spain in canon 3, as found in Gonzales, col. 314.

Section 4. The "Aparatus" of Ioannes Teutonicus (1216)

The commentaries previously considered in this study reflect the canonical evolution that was going on in the concept of an ecclesiastical office. What began as a purely ministerial notion of the functions and the exercise of power inherent in sacred ordination soon developed into a broader concept. The root of this development seems to have been the delineation of the source and extent of the governmental authority bestowed by Christ upon His Apostles and their successors in office. It will be recalled that for Rufinus the episcopal authority consisted in the *lex dioecesana,* which was nothing more than a ministerial power with a concomitant right of visitation and taxation, and in the *auctoritas,* an exclusive ruling authority, or a jurisdictional capacity as such. Some of the same terminology is employed by Ioannes Teutonicus, but it is immediately apparent that further qualifications in these concepts had occurred in the intervening years. For example, the concept of the *lex dioecesana* no longer implied a purely ministerial capacity, since it had come to signify also the rights of collecting the diocesan revenues as well as the right of convoking synods. It thus implied an intrinsic legislative capacity in the holder of an episcopal office.[33]

To supplement this notion, however, Ioannes Teutonicus introduced an entirely new idea in what he termed the *lex iurisdictionis*:

> ... lex iurisdictionis est qua episcopus potest clericos ordinare, altaria et ecclesias et virgines consecrare, corrigere, suspendere, cognoscere de causis civilibus et criminalibus et generaliter ad suam iurisdictionem pertinet omnia sacramenta conferre.[34]

It is immediately apparent that the notion of ministerial

[33] *Glossa ordinaria,* ad C. X. q. 1, c. 1, s. v. *quidam laicus*: "... est autem lex dioecesana qua episcopus recipit cathedraticam, tertiam vel quartam partem decimationum secundum diversas consuetudines, et qua vocat clericos ad synodum vel exsequias ..."

[34] *Loc. cit.*

power has been removed from the concept of the *lex dioecesana* and thus has become part of the *lex iurisdictionis*. The concept of orders and the concept of jurisdiction, therefore, were collected together in one specific notion. This confusion of powers was to breed considerable difficulty for future canonists, and was not to be settled satisfactorily until some years later.

More important than this, however, was the introduction of judicial and coercive capacities into the concept of jurisdictional authority. Through this the bishop became the arbiter of all contentious and criminal actions within the confines of his diocese. This jurisprudential development seems centered around a discussion of the competence of the various curial officials. Of particular concern to our Glossator were the actions brought against clerics.[35] It was his opinion, in following Huggucio, that only bishops possessed the authority and the power to hear and decide the causes of clerics. He based his proof upon the fact that bishops alone were competent to perform jurisdictional acts, since they alone had the power to excommunicate,[36] as well as to hear matrimonial causes.[37]

Ioannes Teutonicus noted, however, that the contrary view could also be supported. In proof of this contention he distinguished between the ordinary and delegated authority exercised by tribunals. Thus a judge did not exercise ordinary power, and therefore was not called a *iudex ordinarius*, unless he had been chosen by a chapter. The implication was that the chapter as a unit possessed ordinary jurisdiction,[38] and through the exercise of its franchise transferred that power to the one so elected. A judge chosen by the faithful (*consensus populi*)[39] or by way of some

[35] The jurisprudence detailed here is taken from the following *glossae*: *glossa ordinaria*, ad C. XI, q. 1, c. 15 (JK, n. 964), s. v. *presbyterorum*, et c. 38 (JE, n. 1912), s. v. *non ab alio*.

[36] C. XVI q. 2, c. 1.

[37] C. XXXV, q. 6, c. 10; Compilatio IV: V, 10, c. un.

[38] C. XV, q. 4, c. 1; Compilatio I: I, 23, 3; III, 36, 4.

[39] D. XCIII, 24, *in fine*.

established customary procedure[40] was not a *iudex ordinarius,* since his electors were incapable of transferring such power.

For an assured effectiveness in this judicial capacity the bishop was also conceded the right to coerce the contumacious through his inflicting of both spiritual and temporal penalties.

In the view of Ioannes Teutonicus, then, the Church was administratively ruled by bishops who received their status or office by reason of their participation in the powers, ministerial and jurisdictional, that Christ left to His Church. It is important at this point, however, to understand that the lines of demarcation between these capacities and exercises of power were not notably incisive, for as our Glossator remarked: "... quandoque lex dioecesana comprehendit etiam legem iurisdictionis."[41] To illustrate this perplexing condition he noted that all churches and monasteries are subject to the *lex iurisdictionis,*[42] but only seculars are subject to the *lex dioecesana,*[43] whereas regulars along with their churches and monasteries were never thus subjected.[44] Needless to say, it was to be the task of future canonists to establish the definition and the limitations of these powers in the episcopal office.

Article 4. Exemption And Episcopal Authority

Relative to the previous article it seems advantageous at this point to consider briefly the established limitations in the episcopal power as detailed by the Decretists. The principal restriction was concerned with religious and their rights of exemption.

> An per episcopum abbas sit eligendus et instituendus. Et quidem non per eum est eligendus, sed per monachos; instituendus est autem, i. e., in electione

[40] C. IX, q. 3, c. 8.

[41] *Glossa ordinaria,* ad C. X, q. 1, c. 1, s. v. *quidam laicus.*

[42] For example: C. XVIII, q. 2, c. 1, c. 17, c. 19; C. XVI, q. 1, c. 10.

[43] C. X, q. 1, c. 8.

[44] For example: C. X, q. 1, c. 1, c. 16; C. XVI, q. 1, c. 34.

> confirmandus, per episcopum. Excipiuntur privilegiata monasteria, quae ab omni iurisdictione[45] episcopi sunt libra, in quibus abbates et reliqui rectores per monachos eliguntur et instituntur.[46]

Here the commentator dealt with exempt religious who were outside the pale of episcopal jurisdiction, and, apart from any and all episcopal authority, possessed not only the common right to elect their superiors, but also the privilege of installing them in office. Not only were they exempt in this way, however, but even their ecclesiastical goods, such as their chapels, housing facilities, etc., were also free from any type of episcopal administration.[47] This, however, was normally granted only by special privilege from the Apostolic See, for otherwise chapels owned by monasteries remained subject to the episcopal authority.[48]

Article 5. The Jurisdictional Powers of the Archdeacon

In a previous article were outlined the developments in the concept of the episcopal office. A somewhat similar unfolding of doctrine can be gleaned from a study of the archdeacon's office. Ioannes Teutonicus in a gloss to the words *et iurgia* in the twenty-fifth Distinction instituted a rather lengthy treatise on the jurisdictional powers of the archdeacon, arguing the pros and cons as to whether this curial official possessed ordinary or delegated jurisdiction as an essential constituent of his ecclesiastical office.

[45] This is the only instance the writer has found in the *Summa* of Rufinus where the term *iurisdictio* is used in this specific sense.

[46] Rufinus, *Summa,* ad C. XVIII, q. 2, s. v. *secundum vero* (Singer, p. 377).

[47] Rufinus, *Summa,* ad C. X, q. 1, c. 1, s. v. *si ex laicis* (Singer, p. 301), et ad C. XVI, q. 1, s. v. *quod monachi* (Singer, p. 353): "... Excipiuntur quaedam monasteria privilegiata, cum habeant baptisterium, habent consequenter et ius dioecesana; quibus monasteriis licet publice baptizare, decimas exigere, sepulturas celebrare et cetera similia facere."

[48] Rufinus, *Summa,* ad C. XVI, q. 2, s. v. *de capellis* (Singer, p. 357).

The commentator's use of the term *iurisdictio* here as elsewhere in his *glossae* should be noticed. It appears from a study of the sources and commentaries thus far that the term *iurisdictio* as such reflected simply the judicial and coercive facets of jurisdictional power.[49]

Ioannes Teutonicus introduced his treatise with the distinction between ordinary and delegated jurisdiction. Since this distinction was to play such an essential role in the jurisprudence on ecclesiastical offices, it will prove advantageous to analyze thoroughly the doctrine here proposed by this glossator.

He began by pointing out that the sources were not definitive: on the one hand the texts indeed seemed to indicate that the archdeacon had ordinary power,[50] but on the other hand, in actual practice, he appeared to act with delegated authority.[51] It was this glossator's opinion, however, that the archdeacon possessed ordinary jurisdiction. With this in mind, then, he set forth his proof by using the text of the *Decretum,* of the *Corpus Iuris Civilis,* and of the decretals of Alexander III (1159-1179) as source material.

The first reason alleged by him concerned an archdeacon who exercised an authority that was not his *ex officio,* namely that of appointing pastors with the *cura animarum.*[52] Ioannes Teutonicus saw in this practice as established by custom an exercise of ordinary rather than delegated power, even though Alexander III forbade the archdeacon in question to exercise this faculty in the future without the mandate of his bishop.[53]

Secondly, the archdeacon was asserted to be a vicar of

[49] Proof of this conjecture is evident from a study of the gloss under consideration as well as the *Glossa ordinaria,* ad D. XXI, 6, s. v. *maiores,* et s. v. *ex ore;* et ad C. XI, q. 1, c. 15, s. v. *presbyterorum;* et *ibid.,* c. 38, s. v. *non ab alio.*

[50] D. LXIII, 20; Compilatio I: V, 32, 3.

[51] C. XVI, q. 7, c. 18.

[52] Compilatio I: I, 15, 4; JL, n. 13898; Mansi, XXI, 1089.

[53] "...Mandamus quatenus ut nemini sine licentia et mandato episcopi curam praesumans committere animarum."

the bishop,[54] and therefore could not possess ordinary power. Perpetual vicars, however, of churches[55] as well as vicar-judges did possess ordinary power.[56] Vicarship, then, did not necessarily imply a purely delegated jurisdictional authority.

The contrary view, however, namely that the archdeacon exercised only delegated power, could likewise be established from the sources, as the glossator noted.[57]

Ioannes Teutonicus concluded his discussion by citing the opinion of Huggucio, who maintained that the archdeacon possessed a limited type of ordinary jurisdiction, since "...eam non potest exercere sine auctoritate episcopi." Huggucio compared this authority with the right to perform episcopal consecrations, as it was exercised by metropolitans, which right nevertheless could not be practiced except in communion with other bishops.[58]

Thus the glossator treated of the powers inherent in the archdeacon's office. The archdeacon was indeed an official, other than the bishop, whose ecclesiastical office presupposed both ministerial and jurisdictional powers. This was truly an evolution in doctrine which differentiated it from what was contained in the *Decretum* and the other commentaries thus far studied.

ARTICLE 6. PENAL LEGISLATION

One final consideration remains in the discussion of the commentaries of the Decretists. As it has been previously pointed out, penal legislation is a source which reveals

[54] Compilatio I: I, 15, 2

[55] Compilatio I: III, 5, 14.

[56] Dig. I, 21, 4; 5; C. I, 50, 1.

[57] *Glossa ordinaria*, ad D. XXV, 1, s. v. *et iurgia*: "... videtur quod habeat delegatam iurisdictionem, quia appellatur ab ipso ad archiepiscopum ut Compilatio I: III, 5, 9; sed si haberet ordinariam iurisdictionem, gradatim fieret appellatio ut C. II, q. 6, c. 28. Item alia ratione videtur hoc, quia tantum de huimiloribus negotiis cognoscit, ut hic dicitur: ergo, est pedaneus iudex ut in C. III, 3, 5; sed pedanei iudices delegati sunt, ut in C. III, 3, 4.

[58] D. LXIX, 1.

considerable information concerning the concept of an ecclesiastical office. It offers indeed but a negative approach; nevertheless this approach is a valid and often a quite fruitful one.

The text of the *Decretum* lists two specific penalties, namely, deposition and suspension, which were applicable to delinquent clerics. The text itself did not distinguish between these two. As a result of this the reader could wrongly suppose that they were identical in effect, and therefore only different modes of expression for the same penal remedy. Rufinus, however, distinguished between them, and in so doing shed considerable light on the Church's penal legislation in the Middle Ages, and indirectly clarified the concept of an ecclesiastical office.

Basically the two penalties were the same. They differed, however, in their duration and in the extent of the punishment imposed as also in the manner in which they were to be inflicted. Rufinus entered into an important discussion of the sacerdotal "office" in his treatise on the penalty of deposition.[59] He noted that it is essentially constituted of two elements: the sacerdotal powers, and the use of those powers. Again, these "powers" are the subject of a basic trichotomy, a division which is essential to a correct understanding of the Church's penal legislation for clerics. In the first place, there is the sacramental power (*potestas aptitudinis seu sacramentalis*), of which a priest can never be dispossessed by any power or sanction except death. There is also his sacerdotal dignity (*potestas habilitatis seu dignitatis*), or what might be termed in a broad sense as his status or office; and finally there is his priestly integrity (*potestas regularitatis*), founded in his good repute, knowledge, etc.

To illustrate this jurisprudence, Rufinus then applied these elements to the penalties of suspension and deposition. Thus, when a cleric committed a criminal act, he lost his good repute in the community (*potestas regularitatis*), but

[59] Rufinus, *Summa,* ad C. I, q. 1, c. 30, s. v. *si iustus* (Singer, pp. 210-11).

he still retained the basic rights and powers he needed for fulfilling his office. Upon being suspended, however, he not only lost his priestly integrity, but also the right to exercise the functions in his orders (*usus officii*) ; and finally a deposed priest not only forfeited the *potestas regularitatis* and the *usus officii,* but also the *dignitas officii;* in other words, he was stripped of everything except the sacramental character conferred upon him in ordination. The liturgical rite that surrounded this awful penalty pointed up for the cleric his utter degradation:

> ... depositio non absque aliqua solemnitate fiet; quippe si presbyter aut diaconus fuerit deponendus, congregatis aliis sex vel tribus episcopis ea tunc eis episcopus solemniter auferet, quae in propriis ordinibus susceperunt, e. g., si presbyter, perdet orarium et planetam, si diaconus, orarium et dalmaticam ... Suspensio vero fit sine celebritate, simpliciter officium episcopo interdicente ...[60]

Of practical moment to this study is the repeated identification of office and the power of orders. A deposed cleric was to be deprived of the symbols of his ministerial office *in perpetuum* as a degradation and sign that he was dispossessed of his ecclesiastical office, whereas the cleric under suspension was forbidden the exercise of the *divina officia* only for the period of time specified by his bishop.[61]

[60] Rufinus, *Summa,* ad D. XVIII, 9, s. v. *presbyter* (Singer, p. 66).

[61] There is yet another Decretist's commentary which might have been included in this study. It is the work of Stephen of Tournai (1128-1203), completed around the year 1160. (*Die Summa des Stephanus Tournacensis über das Decretum Gratiani,* ed. by J. Friedrich von Schulte [Giessen: Verlag von Emil Roth, 1891]). After a careful analysis of this work thus far edited, the writer decided not to discuss it, since it contributed nothing new. In fact, any doctrine applicable to this study was found to be a verbatim statement from Rufinus' commentary.

CHAPTER IV

THE CONCEPT OF AN ECCLESIASTICAL OFFICE IN THE *DECRETALES GREGORII IX* (1234)

ARTICLE 1. PRELIMINARY REMARKS

The next step in the analysis of the constituitive elements in the mediaeval concept of an ecclesiastical office will naturally revolve around the compilation of the illustrious Spanish Dominican canonist, Saint Raymond of Peñafort, known to posterity as the *Decretales Gregorii IX*.

Almost a century had passed since the monumental work of Gratian had been introduced into the law schools of Europe. During these years the legal sciences were developing under the watchful eye of the Apostolic See in cooperation with the schools at Bologna, Paris, and elsewhere. Truly the *Decretum Gratiani* ushered in a new epoch in canonical jurisprudence. The *Magister* himself had synthesized all canon law of previous generations. This, however, was not to be his greatest contribution; rather, his development of canon law into a systematic science was to leave its mark on all future canonical studies. As a result the ecclesiastical legal sciences were born and the great schools which were to foster and develop them blossomed forth in mediaeval Europe.

Canon Law, however, did not remain dormant. It was a practical science, constantly unfolding and evolving. The Church was broadening its frontiers, and bringing all life under its watchful care. Paralleling this came a similar development in the practical running of the Church. The Roman Curia was constantly besieged to solve the difficulties arising in the various dioceses. The Roman Pontiff set about solving these problems through his decretal letters to the bishops who sought his counsel. These letters eventually began to form a supplementary body of ecclesiastical discipline, not that new legislation was necessarily always involved, but rather that a new approach in canonical jurisprudence was evolving.

Eventually these decretal letters were collected by various masters in the schools as well as other canonists (e.g., by Ioannes Teutonicus, Bernard of Pavia, and Bernard of Compostella) and were used in the schools as texts supplementary to the Master's *Decretum.* Some of these collections came to be known as the *Compilationes Antiquae,* or the *Extravagantes,* since they contained the law which was not a part of the *Decretum Gratiani.* In all there were five of these collections which preceded the publication of the *Decretales Gregorii IX.* The last of these was an authentic collection sent by Gregory's immediate predecessor, Honorius III, to the school at Bologna with the Bull of promulgation *Novae Causarum* of May 2, 1226.

It is quite easy to see then how these varied compilations of canonical legislation could produce a mass of confused thinking because of the duplication of sources and the multiplicity of norms established by the developing curial practices.

At the death of Honorius III, therefore, his nephew, Cardinal Ugolino, who as Gregory IX succeeded him, set about immediately to remedy this situation. A canonist himself and once also a professor at the University of Bologna, the new pontiff, early in his reign, even though an old man of 82, gave serious thought to the codification of the existing canon law. This momentous task he entrusted to Raymond of Peñafort, directing him to form a new collection from all pre-existing compilations.

After four years (1230-1234) of serious study and work the new compilation of canon law was finally completed. On September 5, 1234, with the Papal Bull, *Rex Pacificus,* the new collection was officially promulgated and sent to the schools at Bologna and Paris. The document of promulgation eloquently speaks of the conditions of the times and the place which the new compilation was to have in the law of the Church.

> ... Sane diversas consuetudines et decretales epistolas praedecessorum nostorum, in diversa dispersas volumina quarum aliquae propter nimiam similitudinem, et quaedam propter contrarietatem, nonnullae etiam propter sui prolixitatem, confusionem inducere videbantur, aliquae vero vagabantur extra volumina supradicta, quae tamquam incertae frequenter in iudiciis vacillabant, ad communem, et maxime studentium, utilitatem per dilectum filium fratrem Raymundum, capellanum et poenitentiarium nostrum, in unum volumen (rescatis superfluis) providimus redigenda, adiicientes constitutiones nostras et decretales epistolas, per quas nonnulla, quae in prioribus erant dubia, declarantur. Volentes igitur, ut hac tantum compilatione universi utantur in iudiciis et in scholis, districtius prohibemus, ne quis praesumat aliam facere absque authoritate sedis apostolicae speciali ...

It should be remarked here that the collection known as the *Decretales Gregorii IX* is not to be considered as a scientific codification of canon law; it is to be viewed rather as a practitioner's handbook. Therefore, when one is occupied with the problem of trying to establish some particular institute of law, as for example an ecclesiastical office, it is not to be expected that a canonical treatise on this or any other institute will be found in the text, rather one must be contented with analyzing basic canonical problems and decisions as found in the pontifical rescripts in order to arrive at a correct solution of the question at hand.[1]

ARTICLE 2. THE GENERICUSE OF THE TERM *Officium*

Section 1. The Liturgical Sense

It is readily admitted by most canonists that the concept of an ecclesiastical office has never been very precisely de-

[1] For further details on the development of the Decretals see: Alphonsus Van Hove, *Prolegomena ad Codicem Iuris Canonici*, editio altera auctior et emendatior (Romae: H. Dessain, 1945), pp. 357-61 (hereafter cited *Prolegomena*). Alphonsus H. Stickler, *Historia Iuris Canonici Latini* (Augustae Taurinorum: Apud Custodiam Librariam Pontif. Athenaei Saleciani, 1950), pp. 237-251.

fined. At different periods in history the term has had various connotations. Since it is a rather generic concept in itself, one can easily understand how this would naturally result. This is especially true in ecclesiastical parlance, where one finds that the concept is used not only in a juridical sense, but likewise in a liturgical sense.

As far back as the writings of Saint Isidore of Seville and Saint Ambrose[2] one notes that the term, in some instances at least, came to signify a liturgical action. The Mass, sacraments, etc., were referred to as *"divina officia."* This rather loose usage of the term occurs in the Decretals as well. In fact, Saint Raymond devoted one title of the third book precisely to this.[3]

In like manner the term pointed to the canonical hours which every cleric was bound to recite. In the words of the IV General Council of the Lateran (1215):

> ... Haec igitur et similia sub poena suspensionis penitus inhibemus, districte praecipientis in virtute obedientiae ut divinum officium nocturnum pariter et diurnum, quantum eis dederit Deus, studiose celebret pariter et devote.[4]

Section 2. "Officium" as a Trust

The concept of an office has another signification in decretal legislation. In these instances the sense seems to be one of some trust, service, or function attached to an occupation or position. To illustrate this, the following chapter might be cited:

> ... monachi possunt ad ecclesiarum parochialium regimen in presbyteros ordinari, ex quo debent praedicationis officium (quod privilegiatum est) exercere ...[5]

[2] *MPL,* XIV, 51 ff; *MPL,* LXXXIII, 738 ff.

[3] X, III, 41: "De celebratione Missarum, sacramento eucharistiae, et aliis divinis officiis."

[4] X, III, 41, 9, which is canon 17 of IV Lateran as found in Mansi, XXII, 1006. The glossator's notation at the words *studiose et devote* in this text are worthy of note: "... studiose ad officium oris, i.e., sine syncopa. Devote, quantum ad officium cordis ..."

[5] X, III, 35, 5, which is a decretal letter of Innocent III as cata-

The gloss at this place seems to imply that the preaching office as such was a position of trust and ministration conferred upon a worthy candidate by an act of delegation of power, since either the bishop or the Holy See had to intervene. It should be noted here that this concept of an office does entail a participation in the ministerial as well as the magisterial authority which Christ gave to His Church at its foundation. It is not, however, too specific since it involves only one facet of these powers.

Somewhat similar to this is the canonical visitor's office, which is mentioned at various places in the decretals.[6] This functionary, in virtue of power delegated either by the Apostolic See or by the ordinary of the place, conducted the canonical investigation of the diocese to which he was assigned, thus participating in a limited way in the papal or episcopal authority of the grantor.[7]

Section 3. The Office of the Coadjutor

Yet another aspect in this generic concept of an ecclesiastical office can be gleaned from an analysis of several of the decretals under the title: "De clerico aegrotante vel debilitato."[8] At this place Saint Raymond was concerned with the rector of a church or with a bishop who has been stricken with leprosy. One can easily imagine the position occupied in society by those who were afflicted with this horrible malady. The compiler began with a decretal of Lucius III (1181-1185):

> De rectoribus ecclesiarum leprae macula usque adeo infectis, quod altari servire non possunt nec sine magno scandalo eorum qui sani sunt eccle-

logued in Potthast, n. 1329. *Glossa ordinaria*, s. v. *privilegiatum*: "In hoc est privilegiatum officium praedicandi: quia nemo debet praedicare, nisi ei sit commissum ab Episcopo loci, vel ab apostolica sede (X, V, 7, 13) et illi qui per electionem ad hoc eliguntur."

[6] For example, in X, I, 3, 26: "... cui visitationis officium in civitate ac dioecesi Bononiensi commisimus."

[7] Another office of this type is the *officium legationis*. For details see X, I, 41, 5, and X, III, 5, 37.

[8] X, III, 6.

> sias ingredi, hoc volumus te tenere, quod eis dandus est coadiutor, qui curam habeat animarum et de facultatibus ecclesiae ad sustentationem suam congruam recipiat portionem.[9]

It seems that this *vicarius adiutor* was charged with the administrative duties in the church, since its ailing rector was unable to carry them through. The institution of this adjutant provoked considerable discussion among the commentators, as the glossator noted. Huggucio († 1210)[10] was of the opinion that an injustice was done to the rector, since he was in no way responsible for his incapacity, "... ita sine culpa punitur, quod esse non debet."[11] Others made a distinction between bishops and lower prelates. The bishop was not to be removed; he was to be given a coadjutor. Lesser prelates and clerics lower than a bishop were to be removed, and a successor was to be appointed in their stead. Laurentius Hispanus,[12] however, rejected this opinion. According to him the incumbent remained in office as far as the title to that office was concerned; he was merely to be removed from the actual exercise or administration of the office, and a coadjutor was to be supplied, "... et quod dicit hic ab administrationis officio debet removeri: quod est in actu, sed quo ad ius retinebit officium."[13] This indeed

[9] X, III, 6, 3; JL, n. 14965. The following decretal of Clement III (1187-1191) further defined the role of this parochial adjutant: "... De sacerdote qui divino iudicio, leprae morbo repercussus, in parochiali ecclesia praelationis officio fungitur, dicimus quod pro scandalo et abominatione populi, ab administrationis officio debet removeri, ita quidem, quod iuxta facultates, eccelsiae necessaria, quamdiu vixerit, ministrentur." X, III, 6, 4; JL, n. 16607. The gloss thus explained the *officium praelationis*: "... ergo ille coadiutor videtur esse praelatus, ex quo habet curam animarum."

[10] "Summa Hugguccionis, Pisani, Magistri Bononiensis, postea Episcopi Ferrariensis (1190-1210), maximim momenti est; ante a. 1188 non est absoluta."—Van Hove, *Prolegomena*, p. 435.

[11] *Glossa ordinaria*, ad X, III, 6, 4, s. v. *administrationis*.

[12] "Larentius Hispanus, discipulus Azonis, professor Bononiensis, magister Bartholomaei Brixensis, qui postea verisimilter factus est episcopus Auriensis (Orense) ab anno 1218 ad annum 1248."—Van Hove, *Prolegomena*, p. 443.

[13] *Glossa ordinaria*, ad X, III, 6, 4, s. v. *administrationis*.

was an important development in the mediaeval jurisprudence on ecclesiastical offices. For the first time a scientific analysis of the facets in the notion of a sacred office distinguished the purely functionary element (*in actu, exsecutio officii*) from the canonical concept as such. In other words, the juridic concept of an ecclesiastical office was no longer equivalent to the exercise of ministerial power, it now became a distinct canonical entity, an institute of law existing apart from any mere executory power.

Section 4. "Officium" and "Ordo"

From the earlier examination of the concept of an ecclesiastical office in the *Decretum Gratiani* it was established that, for Gratian at least, *officium* was equivalent to sacred orders and the powers and functions inherent in this sacrament. This same signification finds expression in the decretals as well. A decretal of Clement III (1187-1191) to the archbishop of Ravenna bears this out:

> Significavit nobis R. archipresbyter Sancti Stephani, quod B. presbyter (credens se obsequium praestare Deo) fecit sibi virilia amputari, *et infra.* Quocirca mandamus (quatenus si iam dictum presbyterum alias Deo dignum inveneris, ei sacerdotale officium absque altaris ministerio), authoritate nostra fretus et tua, prout videris expedire, concedas.[14]

Another instance wherein this same sense is employed occurs in a decretal of Eugene III (1145-1153).

> Presbyterum cuius digitos cum medietate palmae a praedone abscissos significasti, missam non permittimus celebrare: quia nec secure propter debilitatem nec sine scandalo propter deformitatem membri hoc fieri posse confidimus. Ipsum autem

[14] X, I, 20, 4; JL, n. 16591. *Glossa ordinaria,* s. v. *officium*: "Sicut baptizare, poenitentiam dare, et alia officia praeter officium Missae, et alia similia, quae solis sacerdotibus sunt concessa." The rubric to the text read: "Sacerdos qui sine causa virilia sibi fecit abscindi, credens inde merei, de dispensatione episcopi suum officium (praeter altaris ministerium) poterit exercere."

ceteris officiis sacerdotalibus fungi minime prohibemus.[15]

ARTICLE 3. SOME TYPICAL MEDIAEVAL ECCLESIASTICAL OFFICES

In the following article an analysis of certain ecclesiastical offices which are mentioned in the *Decretales Gregorii IX* is presented. This does not propose to be a comprehensive treatment of these ecclesiastical positions, but rather one which attempts to show their nature. The writer has also omitted in this context any localized customary developments, thus limiting the statement to the common law definition of these offices. Having established the essential elements that constituted these offices, one should then be able to formulate a definition of this canonical institute at this period in history.[16]

[15] X, III, 6, 2. See also: X, I, 11, 10; X, I, 11, 13; X, I, 12, c. un.; X, I, 13, 1; X, I, 14, 15; X, I, 20, 6; X, I, 21, 6; X, I, 37, 3; X, III, 34, 9.

[16] X, I, 23—X, I, 28. The source of some of these chapters remains an enigma to the historian:

Compilatio I	*Collectio Lipsiensis*	*Collectio II Parisiensis*
Ex libro Romani ordinis	eadem inscriptio	eadem inscriptio
"Ut archidiaconus . . ."		
I, 15, 2	33. 1	5. 1
(X, I, 23, 1)		
Ex concilio Toletano	eadem inscriptio	eadem inscriptio
"Ut archipresbyter . . ."		
I, 16, 1	33. 6	6. 1
(X, I, 24, 1)		
Ex libro Romani ordinis	eadem inscriptio	eadem inscriptio
"Ut primicerius . . ."		
I, 17, c. un.	33. 10	7. 1
(X, I, 25, c. un.)		
Ex concilio Toletano	eadem inscriptio	eadem inscriptio
"Ut sciat scarista . . ."		
I, 18, c. un.	33. 11	8. 1
(X, I, 26, c. un.)		
Ex libro Romani ordinis	eadem inscriptio	eadem inscriptio
"Custos ecclesiae . . ."		
I, 19, 1	33. 12	9. 1
(X, I, 27, 1)		

Section 1. The Archdeacon

One of the principal offices which canonical legislation established in order to furnish assistance to the bishop in carrying on the work of the Church was that of the archdeacon. The term itself is derived from the Greek, and means the first or chief among the class of deacons. The term itself is used in Christian antiquity. At that time the archdeacon assisted the bishop in administrative work, and presided over the College of Deacons, a remnant of the Apostolic Church.[17] Gradually his duties were augmented. They consisted in attending the bishop at the altar, and at ordination, and in assisting him in managing the revenues of the Church and in directing the deacons in their duties. By the twelfth century the office of the archdeacon had become a very important ecclesiastical position, since by that time the law itself has assigned to him a proper jurisdiction.[18] By virtue of his office, the archdeacon of the cathe-

All of these texts are derived from a short treatise in eight chapters on *officia,* which is variously found as an appendix to the *Collectio Anselmo dedicata* (MS Vercelli XV: cc. 1-4, 6-8); Burchard's *Decretum* (Pistoia MS, Cath. Chapter 119: cc. 1-4, 5 frag., 6 separately); Ivo of Chartres' *Panormia*: (Venice, Bibl. Marciana *lat.* IV: 51 [Valentrinelli VIII. 12: cc. 1-5] and which was edited and discussed by A. Gaudenzi, "Il monasterio di Nonantola, il ducato di Persiceta e la chiesa di Bologna," *Bulletino dell' Istituto storico italiano,* XXXVII (1916) pp. 395-404, who wrongly supposes that a lost *Ordo* of Nicholas I (867-872) was the original source. For confirmation see: Stephan Kuttner, "*Cardinalis*: the history of the canonical concept," *Traditio,* III (1945), p. 161, note 30. *Inscriptio* in the Venice MS: "Institutum a ss. patribus et viris apostolicis S.R.E.... ex libro romani ordinis"; Pistoia MS: "Ex libro ordinis romani." The relation of the cited texts to Isidore's letter to Leofred of Cordova (D. XXV, 1) has not been sufficiently examined. Although the spurious chapter on the *archipresbyter* (Compilatio I: I, 16, 1) was incorporated in Gratian's text of the letter, the other chapters, even though they were substanially similar, are divergent enough to rule out any direct interdependence.

[17] Acts, 6.

[18] In mediaeval parlance the archdeacon was quite frequently referred to as the *praepositus* or provost, while his counterpart, the archpriest, was referred to as the *decanus* or dean.

dral church was, next to the bishop, the regular organ of supervision and discipline in the diocese. The duties which were attached to his office centered for the most part in the exercise of the power of jurisdiction.

A decretal of Innocent III (1198-1215) outlines the principal duties of the archdeacon as well as the ambit of his vast powers.[19] He held the major position after the bishop and was his perpetual vicar.[20] He was likewise referred to as the "*oculus episcopi*."[21] This title indicates his close association with the bishop. It was conferred upon him because it was his duty to point out what should be corrected and amended throughout the diocese. The archdeacon was the official superior of the subordinate clergy, since he exercised a certain surveillance over the discharge of the duties which were assigned to these clerics.[22]

The primary duties of the archdeacon were the following: to see to it that the divine offices were rightly performed, to take care of the sacred vessels and the treasury of the church, to restore the churches when this was necessary, to visit those churches which were within the limits of the diocese, to examine the candidates for orders and those who were prepared for appointment to benefices, and to present them to the bishop that they might be approved and instituted in their benefices. The archdeacon likewise possessed some judicial authority in that he could hear and decide the causes of clerics which did not involve grave matters, as well as correct abuses and settle other minor difficulties[23]

Although the archdeacon possessed wide ecclesiastical powers, nevertheless in some instances this power was curtailed. First, the archdeacon could not in virtue of his office make appointments to benefices without the special mandate of the bishop, as one learns from a decretal of

[19] X, I, 23, 7; Potthast, n. 5031.

[20] X, I, 23, 1.

[21] X, I, 23, 7.

[22] *Glossa ordinaria,* ad D. XXV, 1, s. v. *archidiaconi.*

[23] X, I, 23, 1, 3, 6, 7, 9.

Alexander III (1159-1179).[24] Second, the archdeacon could not issue dimissorial letters for those who were about to be ordained.[25] According to Honorius III (1216-1227) the archdeacon did not have jurisdiction over regulars unless general or particular custom attributed such authority to him.[26] Fourth, Alexander III in a decretal to the bishop of Worcester stated that the archdeacon lacked the power to inflict an excommunication.[27]

According to decretal law these jurisdictional powers of the archdeacon extended over the whole diocese. In the mediaeval canonical parlance he must be regarded as having a true *dignitas*, because he had jurisdiction which he was able to exercise in his own name, and in a permanent and stable manner as the perpetual vicar of the bishop.

Normally the archdeacon was not ordained to the priesthood, which was one of the necessary qualifications for the incumbent of the archpriest's office. Although in virtue simply of his orders the archdeacon was lower in rank, yet by reason of his wide jurisdictional powers he was above the other members of the episcopal curia, and thus in this sphere he was truly the *alter ego* of the bishop.

Section 2. The Archpriest

In the Middle Ages the office of the archpriest ranked next to that of the archdeacon. In the early ages of the Church reference is made to a college of priests established in individual churches under the direction of the bishop. With the spread of the Faith and the development of the Church the bishop was personally unable to attend to all the affairs of his office. Consequently, he shared his powers with others. To assist him in caring for the poor, the sick, the orphans, and the widows, an assistant was appointed who became known as the archpriest. The term *archipresbyter* meant the first and worthier among the priests,

[24] X, I, 23, 4; JL, n. 13898.

[25] X, I, 23, 8; Potthast, n. 835.

[26] X, I, 23, 10; Potthast, n. 7723.

[27] X, I, 23, 5; JL, n. 13166.

who presided over and commanded the priests in all matters which pertained to their priestly office. He was in truth the *princeps sacerdotum* and, though he retained simply a priestly rank, he excelled others because of the authority which was conferred upon him.[28] The archpriest of the cathedral church was sometimes referred to as the *decanus* or dean.[29] He was the vicar of the bishop in all matters concerned with the spiritual welfare of the diocese, while his counterpart, the archdeacon, was the vicar of the bishop in all matters connected with the external government and public welfare of the diocese.[30]

In antiquity there was only one archpriest. He was connected with the cathedral church and was known as the urban archpriest or the archpriest of the city. The spread of the Faith meant the enlargement of the diocese and naturally necessitated the appointment of assistants to function in the rural areas. These functionaries who presided over the parishes and priests in the rural districts were known as the rural archpriests.[31]

Many functions were reserved to the urban archpriests. As the *princeps sacerdotum* he ruled all priests having the care of souls. In the absence of the bishop he celebrated

[28] X, I, 24, 1.

[29] X, I, 23, 7; Potthast, n. 5031. See also: *Glossa ordinaria,* ad X, V, 4, 1, s. v. *decani.*

[30] *Glossa ordinaria,* ad X, I, 24, 1, s. v. *subesse*: "Sic videtur quod qui maior est in ordine, subsit minori . . . sed archidiaconus praeest archipresbytero quoad dignitatem, non quoad ordinem.

[31] The II Council of Tours (567), c. 19, speaks of the "*archipresbyteri*" and "*reliqui presbyteri et diaconi et subdiaconi vicani,*" Mansi, IX, 797. Council of Rheims (630), c. 19: ". . . ut in parochiis nullus laicorum archipresbyter praeponatur: sed qui senior in ipsis esse debet, clericus ordinetur." Mansi, X, 597; XI Council of Toledo 675), c. 14: "Necessarium duximus instituere ut ubi temporis, vel loci, sive cleri copia suffragatur, habeat semper quisquis ille canens Deo vel sacrificans, post se vicini solaminis adiutorem: ut si aliquo casu ille qui officia impleturus accedit turbatus fuerit, vel ad terram elisus, a tergo semper habeat qui eius vicem exequatur intrepidus." Mansi, XI, 145. See also: X, I, 24, 4, and canon 8 of the Council of Nantes (IX cent.), Mansi XVIII, 168.

the solemn Mass or commanded it to be celebrated by another. Likewise in the absence of the bishop, he blessed the font, anointed the sick, and solemnly reconciled penitents after consulting the bishop.[32] He was obliged to see that no one died without previously being fortified with the sacraments of Penance and the Holy Eucharist. He also could hear the confessions of all the people of the diocese.[33] On the other hand, the rural archpriest presided over the parochial churches of the country and the other priests having minor titles, assuming in their regard the position of an inspector. All those appointed under him were subject to his supervision; however, it was limited by the bishop, so that he frequently had to refer matters to the bishop[34]

The rural archpriests were able to settle minor affairs which did not require judicial intervention, but all matters of greater import were to be referred to the bishop and were subject to his jurisdiction.

In some localities the urban archpriest possessed a true *dignitas,* even though he was subject to the archdeacon. He had jurisdiction in the internal forum, but lacked jurisdiction in the external forum when the exercise of judicial power was required. Like the archdeacon he was the perpetual vicar of the bishop, and his position by that fact possessed a certain measure of stability.

Section 3. The "Primicerius"

Primicerius, as the term indicates, designated the first in the roster of a particular class of officials. In its ecclesiastical use this name applied to the heads of the various colleges of notaries and judges who occupied an important place in the administration of the Roman church in later antiquity and in the Middle Ages. In reference to the notaries the *primicerius* was the one who first by means of his

[32] X, I, 24, 2; JE, n. 1986.

[33] *Glossa ordinaria,* ad X, I, 24, 3, s. v. *a foria veniunt.* For further details of the urban archpriest's office see: D. XXV, 1, and X, I, 24, 1, 2, 3.

[34] *Glossa ordinaria,* ad X, I, 24, 4, s. v. *referant.*

signature witnessed all official documents. In the decretal legislation, however, one finds that the term *primicerius* designated also a *cantor*, whose duty it was to preside over the chant and the ones appointed for chanting, as well as a *scholasticus*, or the director of the clerical schools.[35]

Gradually other duties were assigned to him in reference to the minor clergy. In choir he took his place immediately after the archpriest, and therefore his office is treated immediately after that of the archpriest. The *primicerius* was the teacher of the deacons and the other minor clergy.[36] He carefully guarded the discipline among the minor clergy. He assumed this obligation in such a way that he bound himself in conscience to render an account for their souls before Almighty God. He assigned the lessons to the lectors, and instructed the clergy assigned to him in the performance of the choir offices. In addition to directing the liturgy, he pointed out the repairs to be made in the churches, directed the composition of the letter for the days of fasting, warned clerics whom he knew to be delinquent, and reported them to the bishop if they failed to amend.[37]

Technically the *primicerius* did not have an independent office as such, for he performed his duties under the supervision of the archdeacon, assisting him in the governance of the inferior clergy, since the archdeacon reserved to himself the care and governance of the major and minor clergy[38]

The place which the *primicerius* occupied in the mediaeval schema of ecclesiastical offices was known as a *personatus*. In this position he enjoyed a certain preeminence over the canons, and a precedence in choir. If particular churches recognized this position as a *dignitas* or merely a simple administrative position, this resulted from customary usage and not from the common law. One finds instances, however, wherein the *primicerius* was referred to as having

[35] Hostiensis (Henricus de Segusio), *Summa Aurea* (Venetiis: Ad Candentis Salamandrae Insigne, 1570), I, 25, 1.

[36] X, I, 25, 1.

[37] *Glossa ordinaria*, ad D. XXV, 1, s. v. *primicerius*.

[38] *Glossa ordinaria*, ad X, I, 25, c. un., s. v. *donet lectiones*.

a dignity, a *personatus*, as well as a simple administrative position.[39]

Section 4. The Treasurer, Sacristan, and Custodian

In the *Decretum Gratiani* as well as in the *Decretales Gregorii IX*[40] one finds legislation on various other offices which were to be established in cathedral churches, namely the offices of sacristan, treasurer, and custodian. The sacristan, also called the treasurer in certain churches, was that minister who was charged with the care of the sacred treasures of the Church, for example, the chalices, patens, candelabra, and other ecclesiastical utensils and vestments. The immediate care of these objects pertained to the archdeacon, but the sacristan or treasurer shared in this trust of the archdeacon.[41]

The custodian was the quasi-minister of the sacristan. He, too, was subject to the archdeacon. His main duties were to care for the less precious utensils used in the divine services, and to prepare the bread and the wine and all other things necessary for the ministry of the altar.

From the nature of the work performed by these officials it is quite clear that they were engaged in merely administrative functions, and since they enjoyed neither jurisdiction nor preeminence, their position was technically referred to as an *officium*.[42]

Section 5. Perpetual and Temporary Vicars

With the passage of time the character and multiplicity of the work that devolved upon bishops and rectors of churches became increasingly burdensome. In fact, it was found that they were not always able personally to handle all the affairs which were entrusted to them. These conditions gave rise in canonical history to the institute of vicarship with its concomitant delegation of authority.

[39] X, I, 2, 8; Potthast, n. 2996.

[40] D. XXV, 1; X, I, 26, c. un.; X, I, 27, c. un.

[41] *Glossa ordinaria*, ad X, I, 26, c. un., s. v. *vasorum*.

[42] *Glossa ordinaria*, ad I, 4, 1, in VI°, in principio.

Those, therefore, who exercised power in the name of another were called vicars. In a particular sense a vicar was one who took another's place and supplied in his place if the one for whom he acted was absent or impeded, had died, or was personally unable to perform his charge for any legitimate reason. Usually a vicar in the ecclesiastical sense was appointed to exercise jurisdiction or spiritual ministration on behalf of others.[43]

Vicars normally consisted of various classes. There were those who were established as such by law, for example the archdeacon and the archpriest. Of the archdeacon it was said: "Ut archidiaconus post episcopum sciat se vicarium esse in omnibus, et omnem curam in clero ... ad se pertinere."[44] In spiritual affairs the archpriest had a similar position under the bishop.[45] Therefore the law itself granted certain powers to the archdeacon and the archpriest, and this power was annexed to their offices without any intervention on the part of the bishop.

There were also vicars of jurisdiction and vicars of spiritual ministration (*in divinis*). This division arose from the functions which these substitutes performed. In general, a vicar of jurisdiction was one to whom jurisdictional authority was entrusted by the Pope, by a bishop, or by a chapter. Vicars *in divinis,* on the other hand, ministered in divine worship, had the care of souls and exercised an office on behalf of another in the performance of the duties inherent in the sacred ministry. Depending upon the stability of their offices, these latter were subdivided into perpetual and temporary vicars. A perpetual vicar *in divinis* was defined: "Perpetuus vicarius dicitur qui canonice a persona ecclesiae et auctoritate episcopi est institutus et

[43] *Glossa ordinaria,* ad X, I, 28, 1, in principio: "Viso de iis qui serviunt ecclesiam nomine proprio, videndum est de iis qui serviunt nomine alieno. Et communiter in isto titulo tractatur de vicariis, qui serviunt in divinis: quamvis in capitulo penultimo tractetur de vicario iurisdictionis."

[44] X, I, 23, 1.

[45] X, I, 24, 1.

certam debet percipere portionem."[46] A perpetual vicar had a permanent position and could be removed only for the causes expressed in law. A temporary vicar, on the other hand, could be removed at the will of the one appointing him.[47]

Manifold duties, physical incapacity, and other similar causes justified the appointment of a vicar. In some cases the law demanded the appointment of a perpetual vicar. For example, if a monk obtained a parish belonging to seculars, a perpetual vicar had to be appointed, since in such a case the monk could not administer the sacraments to his parishioners. This is evident from a decretal of Alexander III (1159-1179) to the bishop of Norwich in England.[48] Whenever a filial church was erected a perpetual vicar had to be appointed.[49] In general, the causes requiring the appointment of a perpetual vicar could all be reduced to the necessity or advantage of the parish involved.[50]

Perpetual vicars held canonically established offices, and therefore could not be removed from their vicarship unless they did something which merited deprivation and deposition from the benefice. Alexander III declared that a perpetual vicar acquired a true title to a benefice.[51] The incumbent of a perpetual vicarship was understood to be beneficed: "... non enim beneficio carere debet dici, cui competentur de perpetuae vicariae proventibus est provisum."[52]

A temporary vicar was instituted only for a time. The law itself recognized certain legitimate causes for the appointment of such vicars. Whenever a church or a benefice had fallen vacant because of the death, the resignation, or the deprivation of its incumbent, a temporary vicar could be appointed until provision for the rector was made.[53] Alexander III and Lucius III (1183-1184) recognized as causes for the appointment of temporary vicars the lack of

[46] *Glossa ordinaria*, ad X, I, 28, 1, s. v. *perpetuos vicarios*.
[47] *Loc. cit.*
[48] X, I, 28, 1; JL, n. 14034.
[49] X, III, 48, 5; JL, n. 15750.
[50] X, I, 28, 1; JL, n. 14034.
[51] X, I, 28, 3; JL, n. 14156.
[52] X, I, 3, 27.
[53] X, I, 31, 4; JL, n. 13822.

required age on the part of the incumbent and the inability personally to administer the benefice because of sickness.[54] Another cause warranting the appointment of a temporary vicar was the fact that the principal rector of a church was not able personally to administer his benefice and needed the assistance of others.[55]

A temporary vicar appointed by the pastor or by the bishop acquired no right or title to the benefice to which he was appointed vicar. Nevertheless, he was entrusted with the care of souls and other parochial functions in the name of the pastor who retained the complete charge of the church. The office of a temporary vicar ceased with the death, the resignation, or the deposition of the principal rector, and was revocable at the will of the person appointing him. No strictly canonical cause was necessary for his removal.

Article 4. The Concept of an Ecclesiastical Office Deduced from Penal Legislation

Throughout the Decretals an appreciable amount of attention is paid to the punishment of delinquent clerics. This article will attempt to resolve the concept of an ecclesiastical office from this penal legislation.

A study of the penal legislation in Gratian's *Decretum* definitely showed an intimate connection between the concepts of *officium* and *sacer ordo,* so much so that when a particular canon spoke of a *suspensio ab officio* it necessarily meant that the delinquent cleric, as punishment for his crime, was to be forbidden to exercise the functions of the orders which he possessed. If occasionally orders were specifically mentioned in connection with the statement regarding the extent of the punishment,[56] this restrictive statement was looked upon as affecting the office also, because of the close connection between office and orders.

Before the twelfth century, ordination was forbidden

[54] X, I, 14, 2; JL, n. 13808, X, III, 6, 2; J., n. 14965.

[55] C. XVI, q. 1, c. 48; JE, n. 1197.

[56] For example: D. XXXII, 10; D. XXVIII, 9.

unless a cleric at the time of the reception of orders was destined for a determined ecclesiastical charge.[57] The reception of orders and the acceptance of an office were complementary aspects of the same thing, and therefore were considered as forming one act. In fact, one might say that the exercise of one's orders and the administration of one's office were, indeed, synonomous.

As time passed it became customary to confer not only tonsure and minor orders but also major orders without a title. Those so ordained were known as *clerici vagi* or *acephali.* To put an end to this practice the III General Council of the Lateran (1179) took a definite stand regarding the title of ordination:

> Episcopus, si aliquem sine certo titulo, de quo necessaria vitae percipiat, in diaconum vel presbyterum ordinaverit, tamdiu ei necessaria subministret, donec in aliqua ecclesia ei convenientia stipendia militiae clericalis assignet, nisi talis ordinatus de sua vel de paterna haereditate subsidium vitae possit habere.[58]

The advent of this new legislation ushered in an entirely new concept of an ecclesiastical office. Whereas previously the powers inherent in holy orders and in the office were considered as one, they came to be viewed as separate and distinct entities, as a result in large measure of the evolving doctrine on jurisdiction, and on its inherence in the very concept of an office. Consequently, clerics delinquent in the exercise of their duties and obligations were thenceforward to be punished, not exclusively with the suspension *ab officio,* but if circumstances warranted it, even with a suspension *ab ordine.*[59]

It should be remembered also that the twelfth century witnessed the final unfolding of the beneficiary system. The Church in keeping with this development added an-

[57] Canon 6 of the Council of Chalcedon (451)—Mansi, VII, 345.

[58] X, III, 5, 4; Mansi, XXII, 220. Innocent III extended this discipline to subdeacons: X, III, 5, 16; Potthast, n. 71.

[59] In this regard see F. Kober, *Die Suspension der Kirchendiener* (Tübingen: Verlag der Buchandlung, 1862), pp. 23 ff.

other penalty which extended to this canonical institute. The suspension *a beneficio* did not arise spontaneously; its growth was rather gradual, paralleling the growth of the concept of an eccelsiastical benefice. It has already been shown how, in the early centuries, clerics obtained revenues from their offices. It has also been shown how the delinquent possessor of an office was punished with a deprivation of his revenues and offerings. It was from this practice that the suspension *a beneficio* took its rise.

The twelfth century, therefore, ushered in an element of accuracy and clarity in reference to suspension which had theretofore been wanting. There was a uniform division of the effects of suspension according to a recognized and well-defined triple category. A comparative study of three penal canons of the III General Council of the Lateran (1179) bears this out:

> ...Illos vero, qui sponte iuramentum de tenendo schismate praestiterint, a sacris ordinibus et dignitatibus decernimus manere suspensos.[60]
>
> Ideoque constiuimus, quod usuarii manifesti nec ad communionem admittantur altaris, nec christianam (si in hoc peccato decesserint) accipiant sepulturam, sed nec oblationes eorum quisquam accipiat. Qui autem acceperit, vel Christianae tradiderit sepulturae; et ea quae acceperit, reddere compellatur, et, donec ad arbitrium episcopi sui satisfaciat, ab officii sui maneat executione suspensus.[61]
>
> ...Clerici sane, si contra formam istam quemquam elegerint, et elegendi tunc potestate privatos, et abl ecclesiasticis beneficiis triennio noverint se suspensos...[62]

[60] X, V, 8, 1, which is canon 2 of the council—Mansi, XXII, 218. See also X, V, 3, 45, for a decretal of Gregory IX using this terminology; Potthast, n. 9671.

[61] X, V, 19, 3, which is canon 25 of the council—Mansi, XXII, 231. For other canons of this council using this terminology see: X, III, 1, 8 (canon 11); X, III, 35, 2 (canon 10); X, V, 4, 1 (canon 15). For the decretals of Alexander III see X, III, 2, 5 (JL, n. 13992); X, V, 3, 19 (JL, n. 14229); X, V, 3, 20 (JL, n. 13914).

[62] X, I, 6, 7, which is canon 3 of III Lateran—Mansi, XXII, 218. See also X, I, 6, 44 (canon 26, IV Lateran).

Needless to say, it is not to be expected that a well-defined demarcation between these various concepts will be found in all instances. Evolution of doctrine is a slow process, and so remnants of the older concept in which an office is identified with the exercise of the functions inherent in holy orders were still to be found. Truly suspension from office restricted the rights flowing from that office, whether or not these were founded on the ministerial or the jurisdictional powers inherent in it. It has been noted before, in reference to the advent of the absolute ordinations, that if a cleric had been suspended from orders, this also included the suspension from office, and vice versa. Accordingly, if there was a suspension from office, this included also a suspension from orders.[63] Later, however, a cleric could be suspended from orders, and then the suspension affected only the orders, and not the office.[64]

It should also be remarked here that jurisdiction and orders came to be considered as separate powers. This is evident from a decretal ascribed to Celestine III (1191-1198).[65] The case had reference to an appeal made against a bishop who had suspended a cleric. This bishop, although lawfully constituted, had not received consecration. The appeal was based on this fact. In response the Pope maintained that, since the bishop had accepted his election, he could fully exercise his powers. As the glossator remarked: "Electus, confirmatus, non consecratus potest exercere quae sunt iurisdictionis, non autem ea quae sunt ordinis episcopalis."[66]

[63] *Glossa ordinaria,* ad X, V, 3, 30, s. v. *secreto.*

[64] *Glossa ordinaria,* ad X, V, 3, 45, s. v. *per trienium:* X, V, 21, 2; X, V, 8, 1.

[65] X, I, 6, 15; JL, n. 16572. Loewenfeld noted that this was really a decretal of Clement III (1187-1191), although Compilatio II: I, 3, 7, and X, I, 6, 15, attributed it to Celestine (1191-1198).

[66] *Glossa ordinaria,* ad X, I, 6, 15, s. v. *transmissam.*

CHAPTER V

THE CONCEPT OF AN ECCLESIASTICAL OFFICE IN THE COMMENTARIES OF THE EARLY DECRETALISTS

A new era in canonical jurisprudence began with the promulgation of the *Decretales Gregorii IX,* for it ushered in the age of the Decretalists. These men, often the masters and professors of law at the great universities, were to spend their lives in the study and exegesis of this text. Their deep knowledge of its meaning enabled them to reconcile, in a masterly way, apparent discordances. Indeed, the Decretalists enriched the science of Canon Law with their learning, and by committing their voluminous studies to writing enabled all future students to appreciate their scholarship and erudition. There is proposed here a study of a few of the earliest of these commentaries of the thirteenth century, so that one may inspect the fully rounded out canonical doctrine on the mediaeval concept of an ecclesiastical office. To neglect them would only result in a defective and inadequate presentation in this thesis.

ARTICLE 1. THE *Glossa Ordinaria* OF BERNARD OF PARMA (CIRCA 1240)

The first Decretalist to be studied is Bernard of Parma, also called Bernard de Botone, born at Parma at the beginning of the thirteenth century. He was a professor of Canon Law at the University of Bologna, where he died in March, 1266. He spent his life in compiling an Apparatus on the Decretals, which eventually was accepted as the *Glossa ordinaria* to that text. In editing his work Bernard availed himself of the many commentaries on the *Compilationes Antiquae.* Among others he cited the *glossae* of Tancred, of Laurentius Hispanus, and of Vincentius Hispanus, and in so doing presented the doctrine of these earlier commentators. Since most of the decretals contained in these earlier compilations were to be incorporated into the Gregorian collection, these commentaries were to preserve the earlier canonical traditions, and thus Bernard of Parma serves as a link between the two.[1]

Section 1. The Episcopal Office

Throughout his commentary Bernard of Parma devoted considerable discussion to the many aspects of the episcopal office. Indeed, it is from this analysis that the most definitive statement on the concept of an eccelsiastical office can be established. He began by noting that the episcopal dignity is indeed an order and participates in the sacramental character of orders. He stressed this doctrine though it stood contrary to the view supported by several earlier authors.[2]

Another interesting development of doctrine concerning episcopal orders derives from the statement which compared with the matrimonial bond the bond that unites a bishop to his diocese. The discussion of the simile, established in patristic tradition, was provoked by a decretal of Innocent III.[3] As the marriage bond (*carnale coniugium*) is indissoluble, so too the bond (*spirituale coniugium*) uniting a bishop and his charge is indissoluble, and can be rescinded only by divine intevention "... divina potestate coniugium spirituale dissolvitur, cum per translationem, depositionem, aut cessionem auctoritate Romani Pontificis (quem constat esse vicarium Iesu Christi) episcopus ab ecclesia removetur."[4] In like manner, as the marriage bond arises out of the contracting consent of the parties, so too the basis of the *spirituale coniugium* of the episcopal office is a spiritual contract. This contract comes into existence at the moment

[1] Stephan Kuttner and Beryl Smalley, "The *Glossa Ordinaria* to the Gregorian Decretals," *The English Historical Review*, LX (1945), pp. 97-105.

[2] *Glossa ordinaria,* ad X, V, 33, 5, s. v. *sui ordinis*: "Episcopalis dignitas est ordo ut D. XXI, 1, et D. LXXXIX, 7."

[3] X, I, 7, 2.

[4] *Loc. cit.*

a bishop is chosen and confirmed in office: "... per confirmationem acquirit electus plenam administrationem et vinculum spirituale contractum est."[5] These contractual formalities, then, establish an inherent capacity in the bishop-elect, so that he can exercise his jurisdictional rights even prior to his episcopal consecration.[6]

This certainly marked a momentous evolution in mediaeval canonical doctrine, since, as previously seen, the earlier commentaries made no distinction between the ministerial and jurisdictional authority intrinsic to the episcopal office. In fact, it was their thought that the governing rights and authority were an integral part of the episcopal order, and consequently not distinct from it. Here for the first time, however, one notes an acknowledgment of this necessary separation of powers.

Bernard of Parma was not satisfied with making this distinction, for he illustrated his doctrine by enumerating the numerous facets which individually make up these episcopal faculties:

> Pertinentibus ad iurisdictionem, puta sicut est iudicare, excommunicare, corrigere, iuramenta recipere a vasallis, confirmare, investire, beneficia conferre, et consimilia quae constituunt in iurisdictione, ut in X, I, 6, 9, et X, I, 7, 1, haec omnia in confirmatione sequitur electus. Ea vero quae sunt ordinis, sicut clericos ordinare, chrisma conficere, depositio clericocrum, benedicere virgines, et ecclesias et altaria consecrare, et similia conferuntur in episcopali consecratione, ut in D. LXVIII, 4, et X, I, 6, 28, et X, I, 7, 2.[7]

Following the lead of previous commentators, Bernard also considered the concepts of the *lex dioecesana* and the *lex iurisdictionis*: "... in quibus legibus consistit totum ius et potestas episcoporum."[8] He introduced nothing new in

[5] *Glossa ordinaria,* ad X, I, 6, 9, s. v. *confirmata.*

[6] *Glossa ordinaria,* ad X, I, 6, 15, s. v. *transmissam.*

[7] *Glossa ordinaria,* ad X, I, 6, 15, s. v. *de talibus.* Bernard concluded this gloss with the following: "... ante consecrationem quasi vidua dicitur ecclesia propter huiusmodi, ut ibi dicitur."

[8] *Glossa ordinaria,* ad X, I, 31, 18, s. v. *de lege iurisdictionis.*

his treatment of these two concepts except for the replacement of the *"dare beneficia"* by the *"datio curae animarum."* In fact, his definition parallels the one that is to be found in the gloss of Ioannes Teutonicus. It is evident, then, that Bernard wished to retain this latter concept of the earlier commentators, even though his own jurisprudence on the ministerial and jurisdictional capacities of the episcopal office was by far more incisive.

Section 2. The "Cura Animarum" of the Archdeacon's Office

An earlier analysis has shown in some detail the essential elements that constituted the archdeacon's office. It has been pointed out that this official was second only to the bishop in the exercise of jurisdictional authority, and that his office was the source whence proceeded the regular supervision and discipline within the diocese.

A new mode of expression for this composite of rights and duties is to be found in Bernard's treatment of this functionary. It will be recalled that Ioannes Teutonicus spoke of the *jurisdiction* of the archdeacon; Bernard of Parma, on the other hand, spoke of the *"cura animarum."* A precise definition of the "care of souls" is not to be found in the sources, but an approximate delineation of the rights inherent in it can be gleaned from the following decretal of Gregory IX to the Archdeacon of Paris:

> ... Sed cum in iure confessus fuerit quod archidiaconus Ambianensis de consuetudine suspendit, excommunicat et absolvit presbyteros et priores, et parochiales ecclesias interdicit, necnon archidiaconus visitat, et inquirit quae viderit inquirenda, et procurationes ratione visitationis recipit, evidenter apparet, quod curam habeat animarum annexam.[9]

It is evident then that the *cura animarum* as exercised by the archdeacon connoted in reality a jurisdictional capacity. It consisted in a judicial and coercive power, as well as in a right of visitation and supervision. It is to be noted,

[9] X, I, 6, 54; Potthast, n. 8306.

however, that this power was really not coextensive with the episcopal prerogatives, since the archdeacon could not commit to another this *cura animarum* unless this special faculty was granted through a special mandate of the bishop, or as the result of an entrenched custom,[10] and so, following Hugguccio, the glossator maintained that the archdeacon's office of itself comprised a circumscribed ordinary jurisdictional power that was entirely distinct from any ministerial capacity.

As in Ioannes Teutonicus, so too in Bernard of Parma a great deal of concerned was evidenced as to whether the archdeacon did or did not possess these powers in virtue of his office.[11] The sources revealed that a considerable amount of customary practice had grown up around the archdeacon's office. The common law granted this official certain prerogatives, but the practice drawn from customary usage had in many places greatly augmented these rights. Bernard summed up the situation quite well in the following gloss:

> Alia autem sunt illa, quae de iure communi pertinent ad archidiaconum, ut X, I, 23, 7, et 9. Alia vero potius habent archidiaconi de consuetudine quam de iure communi: quia visitant et corrigunt de consuetudine, ut in X, I, 23, 10, et X, I, 6, 54, et sic de consuetudine omnia alia iura consimilia intelleguntur . . . Sic ergo iura quae loquuntur di-

[10] *Glossa ordinaria,* ad X, I, 29, 15, s. v. *archidiaconus*: "Archidiaconus vel etiam archipresbyter potest committere curam animarum, sed hoc est quando ab episcopo est eis specialiter concessum, ut in X, I, 23, 4; vel cum aliis hoc obtinet de consuetudine, ut in X, I, 6, 54; X, I, 23, 10; X, V, 31, 2."

[11] *Glossa ordinaria,* ad X, I, 23, 4, s. v. *consuetudinis*: ". . . Huggucio dixit quod archidiaconus de iure communi non habet curam animarum, nisi specialiter ab episcopo demandetur, nec alii potest committere . . . Alii dicunt contrarium, scil., quod habet curam animarum et iurisdictionem, et eo quod episcopus eum instituit, sive per collegium eligitur et per episcopum confirmatur, generalem administrationem cum iurisdictione adipiscitur et facit ad hoc." See also *Glossa ordinaria,* ad X, I, 6, 7, s. v. *archidiaconus*; X, I, 6, 54, s. v. *suspendit*; X, I, 39, 2, s. v. *ecclesiastica sententia;* X, I, 23, 7, s. v. *iurgia.*

> versimode de iurisdictione archidiaconi, intellegenda sunt secundum diversas consuetudines diversorum locorum, ut in X, I, 4, 6.[12]

Thus it can be supposed that the archdeacon, either from the common law or through customary usage possessed an ordinary jurisdictional capacity in virtue of his office. This parallel mode of expression, i.e., *cura animarum* and jurisdiction, should be noted here again, since it was in reference to the episcopal office that the commentators spoke of the jurisdiction of the bishop and at the same time of the *lex dioecesana* and the *lex iurisdictionis* intrinsic to the episcopal office.

Section 3. Institution in an Office and Benefice

Mediaeval jurisprudence considered the two concepts of office and benefice as coextensive. Some of the details concerning this unified concept have already been presented. Now, however, there shall follow a brief analysis of some of the canonical formalities which were to precede the actual possession of the title to a benefice. The III General Council of the Lateran (1179) had once again determined the necessity of a specific title at ordination,[13] thus reestablishing the ancient discipline of Chalcedon.

The significance of this concept of title was thus expounded by Bernard of Parma:

> ... dicitur titulus, ipsa ecclesia, ut titulus Sancti Petri. Unde singuli tantum clerici per singulos tantum titulos sunt ponendi, i.e., ecclesias. Unde in ordinationibus quando vocantur clerici, dicitur talis ad titulum talis plebis. Item titulus dicitur clericatus vel canonicatus in aliqua ecclesia. Unde dicitur intitulari, i.e., inclericari vel canonicari. Et dicitur titulus quilibet ordo ecclesiasticus et quae-

[12] *Glossa ordinaria,* ad X, I, 23, 4, s. v. *consuetudinis.* X, I, 4, 6, rebric reads: "In attribuendis officiis novae dignitatis, serviatur consuetudo vicinarum civitatum, quae si diversa fuerit, servabitur magis rationabilis, et alii non praeiudicans."

[13] X, III, 5, 4. See also: X, III, 5, 16; as well as the *Glossa ordinaria,* ad X, III, 5, 4, s. v. *diaconum.*

> libet dignitas vel praelatio. Unde dicitur quis intitulari in aliqua ecclesia, i.e., ordinari vel praefici.[14]

A cleric then was always ordained under some title, but for the effective execution of this the law established certain canonical procedures. In the event of a vacant benefice there was often to be considered the right of presentation which in varying circumstances likewise determined the right of institution in that benefice.[15]

Normally, however, the canonical possession of an office and a benefice was achieved through institution and investiture:

> ... instituere est spiritualis beneficii vel dignitatis possessionem corporalem tradere, quod spectat de iure communi ad officium archidiaconi, ut in X, I, 23, 9, et X, III, 8, 6, ... investire est ius canoniae vel dignitatis tribuere, quod potest fieri per annulum vel librum, sed per hoc non adipiscitur quasi-possessionem nisi postea corporaliter instituatur.[16]

It was thus that a cleric was established in office, and consequently was granted the right to perform the *divina officia* that integrated his "office,"[17] namely, to preach and to administer the sacraments. His jurisdiction, however, was always limited to the internal forum, unless at the same time he possessed some prelatial dignity, as for example that of a prelate in some collegiate chapter.[18] Then

[14] *Glossa ordinaria,* ad X, I, 6, 54, s. v. *intitulatus.*

[15] For a detailed analysis of this institute see: *Glossa ordinaria,* ad X, I, 29, 6, s. v. *plus iuris;* X, III, 49, 3, s. v. *praesentationem rectoris.*

[16] *Glossa ordinaria,* ad X, III, 8, 4, s. v. *instituatur.*

[17] For example, see *Glossa ordinaria,* ad X, V, 38, 12, s. v. *alieno.*

[18] *Glossa ordinaria,* ad X, I, 31, 3, s. v. *ecclesiastica sententia:* "... illud generaliter traditur, quod quilibet praelatus collegiate ecclesiae, licet subsit episcopo, est iudex ordinarius in plebe sua et habet iurisdictionem cognoscendi et excommunicandi, ut hic dicit et in C. XV, q. 3, c. 1, et in X, II, 1, 2. Et illum dico praelatum hoc facere posse, et talem iurisdictionem habere, qui electus est a collegio vel universitate, X, I, 6, 1, et D. XCIII, 7, et idem intelligo, si praeficiatur collegio vel universitati ab eo qui habet adiminstrationem cum iurisdictione, puta episcopo."

he likewise possessed jurisdictional powers similar to those attributed to the office of bishop and archdeacon, and thus shared with them in the supervision within the diocese.

Section 4. Penal Legislation

As the previous chapter has shown, twelfth-century legislation, particularly that of the III Lateran Council in 1179, did much to clarify the confused pre-existing notions of the Church's penal laws as applied to delinquent clerics. The laws on suspension, however, needed further clarification. This the commentators achieved by gathering together the principles contained therein and from them formulating their canonical doctrine. Bernard of Parma was indeed among these. His *Glossa ordinaria* contains a number of treatises on this specific subject, analyzing in detail the Church's threefold distinction in the penalty of suspension.[19]

The import of the legislation of 1179 was that suspension from office necessarily restricted the rights flowing from that office, either ministerial or jurisdictional or both. The glossator was greatly concerned with the distinction of these two rights inherent in an ecclesiastical office. He remarked that four basic canonical rights were forfeited by the suspended cleric: both the active and the passive role in all elections,[20] the right of being postulated by others,[21] and finally, the right to confer a benefice.[22] Then he continued:

> ... Nonne iudicare et praebendas dare est iurisdictionis? Utique. Numquid suspensus potest huiusmodi iurisdictionem exercere? Dicunt quidam quod episcopus suspensus potest excommunicare, et praebendas dare: et respondent illi, X, III, 8,

[19] The doctrine outlined here is taken from the following *glossae*: *Glossa ordinaria,* ad X, I, 4, 7, s. v. *a suspensis;* ad X, I, 6, 25, s. v. *admiserat;* ad X, II, 25, 9, s. v. *contigeret;* ad X, V, 31, 18, s. v. *inanes.*

[20] X, I, 4, 8; X, I, 6, 16; X, I, 13, 8.

[21] X, I, 5, 1, *in fine.*

[22] X, III, 8, 5.

> 5, quod illi episcopus erat ab officio suspensus et iurisdictione. Sed dicunt, quod canonicus suspensus eligere non potest: quia cum sit suspensus, nihil officii retinet: secus est in praelato ... Alli dicunt et melius quod episcopus suspensus non potest excommunicare, nec interdicere, nec dare praebendas ...[23]

The right to inflict an excommunication, to impose an interdict, and to confer benefices pertained solely to the jurisdictional capacity inherent in the episcopal office, since a bishop could exercise this authority even though he was not as yet consecrated, "... quia plus auferet ei suspensio, quam contulerit consecratio: ut dici consuevit, plus tollit negatio, quam ponit affirmatio."[24] Thus a limitation of the episcopal jurisdictional power was effected through a suspension *ab officio,* although the ministerial powers remained intact. Bernard, however, saw the need of a distinction here. A cleric suspended *ab homine* was totally deprived of any and all jurisdictional capacity intrinsic to his office. Just as one who had been excommunicated could not excommunicate another,[25] so too one who had been suspended *ab homine* could not in turn suspend another.[26] On the other hand, a cleric who has been suspended *a canone* retained certain rights inherent in his office:

> ... Si vero aliquis esset suspensus a canone, puta participando cum excommunicatis, ille talis bene potest eligere, et alia facere quae sunt iurisdictionis, sed elegi scienter non potest.[27]

Bernard of Parma summed up this doctrine with the following: "... quia mitius agitur cum lege, quam cum ministro legis."[28]

Another type of suspension to be noted here is the *suspensio a beneficio.* The intimate connection between this

[23] *Glossa ordinaria,* ad X, I, 4, 7, s. v. *a suspensis.*
[24] *Loc. cit.*
[25] C. XXIV, q. 1, c. 4.
[26] X, V, 31, 18.
[27] *Glossa ordinaria,* ad X, I, 4, 8, s. v. *a suspensis.*
[28] *Loc. cit.*

institute of a benefice and that of an ecclesiastical office has already been studied here, and thus one naturally wonders whether the jurisprudence on penalties will reflect a unified doctrine in reference to the two:

> Et licet isti sint suspensi a beneficio, non impediuntur a divinis officiis. Unde omnia negotia tam spiritualia quam temporalia possunt exercere, et tempora talis suspensionis deberent etiam officiare: quia in poenam talis suspensio introducta est: tamen modicam sustentationem debent tunc habere, ne ex toto egeant.[29]

This penalty, therefore, curtailed the enjoyment of the emoluments flowing from the benefice itself, as well as the economic administration of its goods such as the acts of buying or of selling,[30] but did not in any way affect the status or office of the delinquent.

The combined suspension *ab officio et beneficio* is another example of a penalty to be considered here.[31] It was quite extensive in its impact. In fact, Bernard compared its effects to that of a total excommunication or deposition; for the delinquent was not only deprived of his benefice and sustenance, but was also excluded from the communion of the faithful as well as any spiritual benefits that might be his through his incorporation in the Church.[32]

ARTICLE 2. THE *Commentaria* OF INNOCENT IV (1245)

Sinibaldo Fieschi was born in Genoa. He pursued his juristic studies at the University of Bologna under such learned canonists as Laurentius Hispanus, Vincentius Hispanus, and Ioannes Teutonicus. After completing his school-

[29] *Glossa ordinaria*, ad X, I, 6, 25, s. v. *admiserant*.

[30] X, V, 8, 1.

[31] *Glossa ordinaria*, ad X, I, 6, 43, s. v. *suspenduntur*: "... hic (X, I, 6, 43) privantur officiis et beneficiis, et sic in duobus punitur, quia plus peccant; et ibi (X, I, 6, 7) privati sunt beneficiis tantum, quia minus peccant ibi quam hic ... hic maior poena imponit quam ibi, quia plus offendit qui contra ecclesiasticam libertatem aliquid fecit; sed ibi eligitur persona indigna."

[32] *Glossa ordinaria*, ad X, II 25, 9, s. v. *contigeret*.

ing he stayed on at the university as a professor of Canon Law until 1226, when he was called to be an *auditor litterarum contradictarum* in the Roman Curia. In the following year he was raised to the cardinalate, with the Church of Saint Lawrence as his titular church. After a distinguished curial career he was elected to the Supreme Pontificate in the year 1243. During his reign he composed a splendid *Apparatus* upon the *Decretales Gregorii IX*. Innocent IV prepared this commentary as a private doctor rather than as the supreme legislator of the Church, and by using an exegetical method set forth the canonical teaching outlined in the Decretals. He died December 7, 1254.[33]

Section 1. The Juridical Concept of the "Cura Animarum"

In the previous article there was set forth the concept of the *cura animarum* as possessed by the archdeacon and other minor prelates within a diocese. Innocent IV indicated[34] that this doctrine was really Huggucio's, and that Bernard of Parma followed him in this. His own doctrine, however, disagreed with their opinion. The basis for his contention seems to have risen out of the distinctions then being proposed by the canonists and theologians in the concept of jurisdictional power with specific reference to the internal and sacramental forum.

In attempting a solution of his difficulty Innocent IV distinguished between the concepts of *cura* and of *cura animarum*.[35] According to Fieschi, the concept of *cura animarum* related exclusively to a use of the sacramental powers of absolution, and therefore the *cura animarum* could rest solely with one who was in priestly orders. Thus an archdeacon could not be said to possess the *cura animarum*

[33] Van Hove, *Prolegomena*, p. 477. Bertrandus Kurtschied, O.F.M. and Felix A. Wilches, O.F.M., *Historia Iuris Canonici*, Tom. I, *Historia Fontium et Scientiae Iuris Canonici* (Romae: Officium Libri Catholici, 1943), p. 259. The writer has used the edition *Commentaria in V Libros Decretalium Innocentii IV*, Venetiis, 1570.

[34] *Commentaria*, ad X, I, 23, 4, s. v. *curam*.

[35] *Loc. cit.* et *Commentaria*, ad X, III, 5, 28, s. v. *curam animarum*.

unless he also possessed the sacerdotal character. In keeping with this doctrine Innocent IV also maintained that, even though an archdeacon could bestow a church upon a priest, nevertheless he could not grant to that priest the *cura animarum* unless the archdeacon himself were constituted in priestly orders.[36]

The concept of *cura,* on the other hand, implied a much wider extension of meaning. It served to designate a public power exercised by certain ecclesiastical officials. Its primary purpose was not the forgiveness of sin, but rather the maintenance of discipline and morale among the faithful.[37]

Thus Innocent IV clarified the concept of an ecclesiastical office by incisively distinguishing between the ministerial and jurisdictional powers possessed by certain officials. The *cura animarum* postulated a ministerial capacity, whereas *cura* derived from a jurisdictional authority; both, however, were intrinsic to certain ecclesiastical offices, and as such conferred upon their possessors certain ecclesiastical rights and obligations towards the Church in general as well as to its individual members.[38]

Section 2. "Dignitas" and "Personatus"

Mediaeval parlance developed a definite pattern of desig-

[36] *Commentaria,* ad X, I, 23, 4, s. v. *curam:* "... Quamvis dici posset quod archidiaconus et electi et confirmati et alii huiusmodi, quamvis non sint sacerdotes, tamen possunt dare ecclesias sacerdotibus nec dant curam animarum, sed is, cui dant quando fuit factus sacerdos."

[37] "... large dicitur cura potestas eiiciendi et recipiendi in ecclesiam corrigendi et puniendi excessus. Sub hac cura est excommunicare, interdicere, visitare, etc., quae sunt ad correctionem morum."—*Loc. cit.*

[38] Innocent IV further clarified this distinction in the following gloss: *Commentaria,* ad X, V, 31, 18, s. v. *violare:* "... absolvere excommunicatum per sententiam non est ordinis, sed iurisdictionis, sicut excommunicatio, C. II, q. 1, c. 11. Sed absolutionis solemnia exhibere, sicut dicere orationes cum stola, et psalmum poenitentialem, et in ecclesiam introducere, est ordinis et officii, X, V, 39, 29, in fine ..."

nating the type of office possessed by certain functionaries within the Church. The sources and commentaries reveal the fact that the expressions *dignitas* and *personatus* were often used as equivalent to the concept of *officium*. Normally this terminology was reserved for privileged offices such as canonries in cathedral and collegiate chapters.[39] Fieschi noted the diversified customs so prevalent throughout mediaeval Europe. He mentioned, for example, that an official who was charged with the temporal administration of the church property was normally said to possess a dignity (*dignitas*), while in England this functionary was called a curate (*curatus*). Likewise, in many places abbots and bishops were considered as having only a dignity, and not a *personatus*, even though they did exercise extensive jurisdictional powers. To eliminate this equivocation, therefore, Innocent IV set forth a concise definition of each of these concepts.[40]

A dignity (*dignitas*) implied administrative capacity, either temporary or perpetual. An official who possessed a *personatus*, besides having administrative capacity also had jurisdictional authority. A beneficiary was one who possessed a dignity as well as a benefice with the *cura animarum*.[41] Finally, a charge which lacked any ministerial or jurisdictional authority was referred to as an *officium*.

Section 3. The Transfer and Limitation of Jurisdictional Powers

Although it is evident that certain ecclesiastical offices subordinate to the episcopate possessed a circumscribed jurisdictional authority, nevertheless the transfer of this power to a duly constituted official often posed problems for the canonists. Innocent IV dealt with this question in various sections of his commentary. The normal procedure seemed to be the election to these prelatial offices by

[39] *Glossa ordinaria*, ad X, III, 4, 3, s. v. dignitates, et ad X, I, 3, 15, s. v. *maiores et digniores*, et ad D. XXV 1, *Casus*.

[40] *Commentaria*, ad X, III, 5, 28, s. v. *personatus*.

[41] *Commentaria*, ad X, III, 5, 33, s. v. *ad rectoriam*.

some corporate body (*universitas*) which possessed the right to transfer the power of its governance, as for example, the election to the office of abbot.[42] This transfer of power, however, was always limited by the common law; for although the electors could transfer certain administrative and jurisdictional capacities to the elected, nevertheless they could never convey the right to inflict an excommunication and to impose an interdict.[43] These two powers were intrinsic to the episcopal office only, and in fact were called the *mucro episcopalis*. If the election was carried out under episcopal authority, however, or was subsequently approved by the bishop, then and only then did the elected official possess the totality of jurisdictional authority.[44]

One final point to be noted is that these officials possessed ordinary power. An election, therefore, did not effect a delegation of power. Even the episcopal prerogatives held by these minor officials were considered ordinary faculties and thus were made available for delegation to others.[45]

Section 4. The Episcopal Office

The basic mediaeval concept of the episcopal office has already been sufficiently reported here. It will suffice then to add the few supplemental details that Innocent IV contributed. He reasserted the traditional twofold distinction in episcopal authority. His application of the doctrine was restricted to the governance of parishes within the diocese with specific reference to regulars and their rights of exemption. Through his detailed analysis and application of the various facets of power embraced in the *lex dioecesana* and the *lex iurisdictionis* he established the measure of

[42] *Commentaria,* ad X, I, 31, 6, s. v. *significavit.*

[43] *Commentaria,* ad X, I, 23, 5, s. v. *sententiam*: "... Praelati qui habent tantum iurisdictionem a collegiis, vel aliis quam episcopis, non possunt excommunicare, quia hanc potestaem non potest concedere nisi episcopus, C. XXIV, q. 3, c. 17, ... nam quod non habent, dare non possunt."

[44] "... nisi forte collegium eligeret auctoritate episcopi, vel ab eo confirmaretur."—*Loc. cit.*

[45] *Commentaria,* ad X, I, 31, 3, s. v. *praelatis.*

authority that a bishop could exercise over exempt religious and their churches.[46] He maintained that the privilege of exemption extended not only to the religious themselves, but also to their churches, except for those which were distinctly parochial. In those churches a bishop retained his authority over the vicars assigned to them. This authority he held in such a manner that it was from him that they received their authority to act as well as their very appointment to the office.[47]

ARTICLE 3. THE *Summa Aurea* (1253) AND *Commentaria* (1271) OF HOSTIENSIS

The published studies of still another mediaeval canonist remain to be analyzed here, those of the justly famous Henry of Susa, Cardinal-Bishop of Ostia, and hence called Hostiensis. Henry of Susa pursued his legal studies at the University of Bologna, but did not remain there as many of his predecessors had; instead, he taught at Paris from 1230 to 1240. Sometime between 1250 and 1253 he composed his *Summa Aurea,* a collection of essays briefly expounding the contents of the various titles in the *Decretales Gregorii IX.* Several years after composing this work Hostiensis completed (June 8, 1270-April 30, 1271) his most noteworthy contribution to canonical science, and undoubtedly the most illustrious of all mediaeval canonical commentaries, his *Commentaria* on the Decretals. In this work he set about to expound all of the canonical doctrine contained in each chapter of the compilation of Gregory IX. Hostiensis died in 1271. The exact date is not certain; authors, however, generally point to October 25 or November 6 of that year.[48]

[46] *Commentaria,* ad X, III, 35, 1, s. v. *vendicare.*

[47] *Commentaria,* ad X, V, 33, 7, s. v. *specialiter,* et ad X, III, 35, 7, s. v. *omnino,* et ad X, III, 29, 1 (expositio ad rubricam).

[48] Van Hove, *Prolegomena,* pp. 476, 478. The following editions were used: *Summa Aurea* (Venetiis: Ad Candentis Salamandrae Insigne, 1570) and *Commentaria in Libros Decretalium* (6 vols., Venetiis: Apud Iuntas, 1581). (Hereafter cited *Summa* and *Commentaria*).

Section 1. The Office of an Ordinary

One of the original contributions of Hostensis to mediaeval jurisprudence was his formulation of concise definitions of many canonical concepts, as for example of the concepts of ordinary and delegated authority. Some of the details of the origin and development of these concepts have already been outlined. It was this author, however, who seemed to synthesize all the principles of his predecessors, and through this analysis to set forth the most consistent statement of this doctrine.[49] The mediaeval development of these concepts was usually centered around the judicial authority possessed by various officials within the Church. As has been noted before, the concept of jurisdictional capacity was in its canonical origin identified exclusively with the handling of judicial affairs.[50]

A person was said to hold an ordinary office if in his own right (*iure suo*) or in virtue of some privilege attaching to his benefice he could exercise a universal jurisdiction in the territory and over the subjects committed to his care. The position of delegate, on the other hand, lacked one or the other of these requisites, and thus did not carry with it the possession of ordinary authority.

Normally, then, one was constituted an ordinary in one of three ways: 1) in virtue of a committed exercise of authority. Thus the Pope in appointing Patriarchs or Archbishops constituted these officials as ordinaries with the consequent capacity to act, not simply as his delegates, but rather in their own right; 2) through an election to office.

> ... Item universitas facit ordinarium eligendo ipsum. Potest igitur dici quod omnes ministri ecclesiae qui per electionem creantur, iurisdictionem ordinariam habent ex quo administrationem consequuntur ...[51]

[49] The details here presented are taken from *Summa*, I, 33.

[50] Summa, II, 2, § *qualiter distinguatur*: "... est autem iurisdictio: potestas de publico introducta cum necessitate iuris dicendi, et aequitatis statuendae ..."

[51] *Summa*, I, 33, § *quis possit constitutere.*

and 3) as a result of some entrenched customary practice. This was in particular exemplified in the authority possessed by the archdeacon.

The law likewise established certain requirements. To be an ordinary one necessarily had to be free, and not a serf; of the male sex; and at least twenty years old. Besides, an ordinary had to be prudent and discreet in all his dealings and not in any way infamous. Thus a heretic, a schismatic, or an excommunicate was barred from holding such an office.

Hostiensis then undertook to analyze the constitutive capacities possessed by an ordinary. He summed up the matter thus: "...ut habeant curam animarum suorum." This *cura* certainly implied a very generic concept, but through his subsequent analysis it could easily be established that the notion of this *cura* comprised in reality the totality of all ministerial and jurisdictional powers possessed by individual officials within the Church. Hostiensis also noted the hierarchical grades among those officials, detailing the specific sphere of authority exercised by each, the one subject to the other, and yet no one the delegate of the other.

> ...Sunt autem distinctae iurisdictionis, et gradatim ascendunt et descendunt. Unde Papa superior est omnibus, et legatus post ipsum quantum ad provinciam sibi commissam... postremo archidiaconus qui est iudex archipresbyterorum, archipresbyter presbyterorum, presbyter propriorum parochianorum...[52]

An ordinary, however, though established in office, could be hindered from exercising his authority. The mediaeval canonists maintained that a *suspensio ab officio* was in reality an impediment to the use of ordinary power; likewise, an ecclesiastical official, once he had been excommunicated, could not exercise his prerogatives.

Finally, the possession of an ordinary office was subject to termination in four specific ways: 1) through the death

[52] *Ibid.*, § *quid pertinet ad officium*, n. 7.

of the office holder, "... quia mors omnia solvit"; 2) through resignation from his office; 3) through deposition from it, and 4) through a transfer to another specific assignment.

This doctrine as enunciated by Hostiensis was certainly a clarification in the mediaeval concept of an ecclesiastical office. It must be admitted, then, according to Hostensis, that to be constituted in an ecclesiastical office a person had to participate in some degree in the ministerial and jurisdictional authority established by Christ in His Church.

Section 2. The "Officialis"

An ecclesiastical office of considerable interest in the present study is that of the *officialis.*[53] This functionary was first mentioned in decretal legislation when Alexander III (1159-1181) settled a dispute in the archdiocese of Canterbury over the right to institute clerics in their benefices.[54]

Bernard of Parma had defined his rôle in the diocesan government thus:

> Officiales dicuntur quibus episcopi committunt vices suas, qui possunt instituere vice episcoporum.[55]

Hostiensis recognized this opinion,[56] but took exception to it at the same time. He noted that there were authors who held that the office of the *officialis* was specifically limited to the conferring of benefices, whether this was accomplished *iure suo,* or in virtue of some approved custom, or finally through a special mandate issued to this functionary by his bishop. Taking these details into consideration,

[53] For a comprehensive study of this office see: Paul Fournier, *Les Officialités au Moyen Age* (Paris: E. Plon et Cie., 1880).

[54] X, III, 7, 3; JL, n. 13817.

[55] *Glossa ordinaria,* ad X, III, 7, 3, s. v. *officialium.* Cf. also Innocent IV, *Commentaria,* ad X, III, 7, 3, s. v. *officialium*: "Nomine talium officialium intelligo hic comprehendi omnes ad quos de iure vel consuetudine approbata pertinet collatio, sive fuerit archidiaconus, sive alii, dummodo auctoritate speciali vel generali episcopi faciant."

[56] *Commentaria,* ad X, III, 7, 3, s. v. *ex sequentibus.*

Hostiensis maintained that the office of the *officialis* was identifiable with that of the archdeacon. On the other hand, noting the practice in France and "*in aliis diversis mundi partibus*," he also maintained that this functionary held an ecclesiastical office distinct from that of the archdeacon. Custom then was evolving a new ecclesiastical office.

In defining the authority of the *officialis* Hostiensis stated that he possessed ordinary jurisdiction, and represented the episcopate in all jurisdictional matters within the confines of the diocese. "*Unde et quod ipse fecit, episcopus facere videtur.*"[57] ....

Section 3. The Parochial Office

Mediaeval jurisprudence presents a unique and interesting insight into the concept of an ecclesiastical office in its detailed treatment of the parochial office. It must be remembered that the proprietary church concept was still prevalent in Europe. A parish, according to this theory, was devoid of any juridic personality, it was merely the subject of certain defined rights and obligations. In keeping with this the beneficiary of such a land-holding was called a vicar or rector, charged with the administration of the tenure, and the obligation of caring for the spiritual wants of the faithful attached to it. In return for this service the incumbent was conceded the right to share in the profits accruing from his benefice. The beneficiary was said to have a "*ius percipiendi proventus in ecclesia.*"[58]

Hostiensis defined a parish:

> Locus in quo degit populus alicui ecclesiae deputatus, certis finibus limitatus, et accipitur quatenus spirituale ius ecclesiae se extendit.[59]

He called it a "*locus,*" thus withholding from the notion of a parish the concept of any canonical personality. Subse-

[57] "... officialis is qui ad iurisdictionem pertinent vices episcopi representat."—*Loc. cit.*

[58] Hostiensis, *Summa,* III, 5, § quid sit praebenda.

[59] *Summa,* III, 35, § quid sit parochia.

quently, when dealing with the *ius parochiale*,[60] he regarded it as essentially the liability that devolves upon the rector of a church to minister to the spiritual needs of the faithful. The rector or the vicar, however, assumed the obligation in virtue of his incumbency in the benefice, rather than as a duly constituted official in the Church, and as such then could not be said to hold an ecclesiastical office in the sense that has been outlined here. Nevertheless, the vicar's exercise of the ministerial powers which were his through ordination did confer upon him a circumscribed ecclesiastical status or office. He lacked any and all jurisdictional power, however, except that which he exercised in the internal and sacramental forum.

Section 4. The Formalities Antecedent to Possession of an Ecclesiastical Office

To achieve the complete possession of an ecclesiastical office as well as the right to exercise the canonical rights inherent in it, its recipient had to obtain authoritative approval in his official status. Mention has already been made of some of the formalities outlined in the Decretal legislation, but there may be added here a little a of the detail that Hostiensis contributed in this regard. It is important that the reader keep in mind, first of all, the basic distinction between the ministerial and jurisdictional authority possessed by an ecclesiastical official, and also his rights as an ecclesiastical beneficiary. To the mediaeval canonist this threefold distincton was basic to the concept of any ecclesiastical office.

Logically, then, ordination or consecration was the first step in the establishment of an office, for it was in virtue of the sacrament of orders that a person became sealed with

[60] *Summa*, III, 35, § *in quibus consistit*: "Ius parochiale consistit in cura animarum parochianorum de quibus parochialis sacerdos coram Deo tentur reddere rationem si culpa sua perirent . . . consistit in collatione sacrorum . . . in coemeterio et iure sepulturae, in poenitentiis aduiendis . . . Unde parochiani singulis diebus dominicis et festivis debent ad propriam ecclesiam convenire."

a character that segregated him from his brethren and bestowed upon him certain capacities to perform the *divina officia.*

> Sacramentum ecclesiae ab Apostolis introductum [sic] cuius character per manus impositionem praelati, secundum formam ecclesiae, cooperante Spiritu Sancto, imprimitur ordinato, ut in certis officiis valeat administrare.[61]

It happened quite frequently, especially in the more important offices such as that of a bishop or an abbot, that one was chosen prior to any consecration, blessing or ordination. In this instance the one so elected acquired a *ius* to that office, that is, a canonical right to be ordained and established in office. This *ius* also conveyed to the elected all the jurisdictional and administrative powers inherent in his office, although the *"plenitudo officii"* was necessarily postponed until the time of sacred ordination or consecration.[62]

Supplementing this, all ecclesiastical officials possessed beneficiary rights. Some possessed them in virtue of their appointment to an office, while others were dependent upon an assignment to a specific benefice, and so their offices were not integrated until such an appointment had taken place.[63]

Section 5. An Ecclesiastical Office and Its Inherent Powers

Hostiensis in his *Commentaria* presented the clearest and most definitive statement in all mediaeval canonical literature thus far considered concerning the concept of an ecclesiastical office. Indeed, so the writer thinks, he not only

[61] Hostiensis, *Summa* I, 24, § *quid sit ordo.*

[62] Hostiensis, *Commentaria,* ad X, I, 6, 34; et ad X, I, 6, 5; et ad X, I, 23, 4.

[63] *Commentaria,* ad X, III, 8, 4, s. v. *assignatione*: "... circa quod notandum quod quantumcumque aliquis in canonicum canonice eligatur, in praebenda tamen non habet administrationem nisi sibi primitus assignetur ... Electio enim dat ius canonicatus ... Assignatio autem praebendae, quae consistit, in facto administrandi in ea, tribuit potestatem administrandi."

synthesized all previous expressions of this concept, but he also established in his commentary on the Decretals the common mediaeval doctrine on this basic institute of canon law. His canonical acumen enabled him to distinguish the ministerial and jurisdictional authority inherent in an ecclesiastical office even more incisively than his predecessors.

This study has already demonstrated that a new mode of signifying the concept of jurisdictional power was evolving during the early years of the thirteenth century. In keeping with this the archdeacon was said to possess the *cura animarum* rather than jurisdiction, although this latter mode of expression was still in vogue. Innocent IV, on the other hand, was wont to designate the *cura animarum* as a limited type of jurisdiction to be exercised in the internal and sacramental forum, and so only by one who was in priestly orders.

Hostiensis, however, disagreed with Innocent IV.[64] As he rightly pointed out, *potestas* and *cura* were two distinct concepts. One had a capacity or a power (*potestas*) in virtue of his ordination, that is, one possessed the authority to perform the sacred offices, inclusive of the exercise of the "power of the keys." On the other hand, there were many who possessed a *cura* who did not have any sacerdotal authority (*potestas*), such as the archdeacon, once he was canonically confirmed and instituted in his office.[65] The *cura animarum,* therefore, pertained to the jurisdictional authority possessed by an ecclesiastical office-holder, and was not an integral part of his ministerial rights. The *"potestas clavium,"* however, could be accessory only to the priestly office, even though its exercise might be restricted, since a bishop could limit the use of this power.[66]

The commentator summarized his argument in the following gloss:

[64] *Commentaria,* ad X, I, 23, 4, s. v. *animarum*: "Ego tamen hanc distinctionem non intelligo: etenim potestas ligandi et solvendi in foro poenitentiali cura dici non potest, nec secundum ius: quia hoc nullo iure cavetur, nec secundum rationem."

[65] X, I, 6, 5; X, I, 6, 15; X, I, 14, 5; X, V, 31, 2.

[66] X, III, 40, 9.

> Unde et quando talis praelatus ordinatur, non datur ei cura, quam iam receperat, sed potestas ligandi, atque solvendi animas sibi commissas, quam sine ordine non habebat, quamvis posset alii (sacerdoti tamen) committere, ut easdem in foro poenitentiali audiret et absolveret: quia hoc iurisdictionis est, quam ratione curae habet.[67]

The jurisdictional concepts of the *lex dioecesana* and the *lex iurisdictionis* as inherent in the episcopal office had fallen into dissuetude in Hostiensis' day. In fact, he referred to this doctrine as the "*distinctio antiquorum Doctorum.*" Nevertheless, he chose to discuss these two concepts, and in so doing further clarified the notion of the episcopal office.[68]

In the first place he mentioned that there is a basic distinction between these two: the *lex iurisdictionis,* on the one hand, is an active power that enables a bishop to do or to perform certain ministerial and jurisdictional acts, whereas the *lex dioecesana* is rather a passive potency, a capacity to receive the diocesan revenues that are his in virtue of his office.[69] All previous commentaries had placed the ministerial powers to confer the sacraments within the ambit of the *lex iurisdictionis.* Hostiensis, however, noted the discrepancy, and resolved it by including these ministerial rights within the one concept, the *lex dioecesana,* thus separating this power from the jurisdictional powers possessed by a bishop.[70]

This completes the treatment of the mediaeval canon-

[67] *Commentaria,* ad X, I, 23, 4, s. v. *animarum.*

[68] *Commentaria,* ad X, I, 31, 18, s. v. *ad legem iurisdictionis;* et ad X, III, 35, 1, s. v. *Theodosius.*

[69] *Commentaria,* ad X, III, 35, 1, s. v. *offeri contingit*: "... fit haec mentio de duplici lege in quibus universa episcoporum: lex iurisdictionis consistit in conferendo, scil., in actione, e.g., conferre beneficia, iudicare, privare, etc.... lex dioecesana consistit in recipiendo, i.e., in passione dulci, sicut est tertia oblationum et mortuariorum ..."

[70] *Commentaria,* ad X, I, 31, 18, s. v. *ad legem iurisdictionis*: "... unde melius est quod dicamus quod una lex tantum est, quam habet episcopus in ecclesiis sibi subiectis, scilicet, lex dioecesana, sub qua et lex iurisdictionis et totum ius episcopale comprehenduntur."

ical doctrine on the concept of an ecclesiastical office. An ecclesiastical office, as it was understood in the latter half of the thirteenth century, could be defined as a sacred commission or charge to exercise in one's own name either the proper ministerial functions inherent in the class or grade of orders possessed, or the jurisdictional powers possessed in virtue either of the common law or of the established customary practice, or of both, as well as all of the administrative powers defined by ecclesiastical law as attaching to the said commission or charge.

CONCLUSIONS

1. In canonical texts the earliest usage of the term *officium* was reserved for the liturgical functions and ministerial powers exercised by those participating in the sacrament of orders.

2. Gratian perpetuated this usage and introduced it to the classical period of mediaeval canon law through his use of the letter concerning ecclesiastical offices of Saint Isidore of Seville to Leofred, Bishop of Cordova. (D. XXV, 1).

3. Although early conciliar legislation certainly recognized a circumscribed governing or jurisdictional authority over and above a ministerial capacity as inherent in certain ecclesiastical offices, nevertheless it was the mediaeval canonists who were to develop this doctrine.

4. Following the classical Roman law, early mediaeval jurisprudence reserved the term *iurisdictio* for the judicial facet of jurisdictional power. The totality of this power was referred to as *potestas, auctoritas, lex dioecesana, lex iurisdictionis,* and *cura animarum.* During this early period no incisive distinction was made between the jurisdictional and ministerial powers possessed by ecclesiastical officials.

5. During the Middle Ages the normal exercise of jurisdiction within a diocese was reserved to the bishop and the archdeacon. The analysis of the facets of powers exercised by these officials was instrumental in integrating jurisdictional authority as a part of the concept of an ecclesiastical office.

6. Early in the thirteenth century the canonists clearly distinguished the power of jurisdiction from the concept of the power of orders, and at the same time delineated the threefold legislative, judicial, and coercive powers as integral to the concept of jurisdiction.

7. The ecclesiastical institute of benefice was intimately linked with an ecclesiastical office in mediaeval canon law. *Beneficium datur propter officium.* In fact, most ecclesiastical offices were endowed with some source of revenue.

8. The mediaeval concept of an ecclesiastical office is to be defined as a sacred commission or charge to exercise in one's own name either the proper ministerial powers inherent in the class or grade of orders possessed, or the jurisdictional powers possessed in virtue either of the common law or of the established customary practice, or of both, as well as all proper administrative powers defined by eccelsiastical law as attaching to the said commission or charge.

BIBLIOGRAPHY

Sources

Corpus Iuris Canonici, editio Lipsiensis secunda poost Aemili Ludovici Richteri curas instruxit Aemilius Friedberg, 1879-1881. Editio anastatice repetita, Lipsiae: Tauchnitz, 1928.

Corpus Iuris Civilis, Institutiones, ed. sterotypa 15., recognovit Paulus Krueger, *Digesta*, ed. sterotypa 15., recognovit Theo. Mommsen, retractavit Paulus Krueger, *Codex Iustinianus*, ed. sterotypa 10., recognovit et retractavit Paulus Krueger, *Novellae*, ed. sterotypa 5., recognovit Rudolfus Schoell, absolvit Guilelmus Kroll, 3 vols., Berolini: Apud Weidmannos, 1928-1929.

Decretales Gregorii IX, cum epitomis, divisionibus, et glossis ordinariis, Venetiis, 1567.

Decretum Gratiani, emandatum et notationibus illustratum, una cum glossis, 3 vols., Augustae Taurinorum, 1588.

Institutes Gaii, texte etabli et traduit par Julien Reinach, Paris: Societé d'Edition "Les Belles Lettres," 1950.

Bruns, Hermann T., *Canones Apostolorum et Conciliorum Veterum Saeculorum IV-VII*, 2 vols., Berolini: G. Remerius, 1839.

Breul, Iacobus du, *Opera Omnia Sancti Isidori*, Coloniae Agrippinae: Antonius Hierat, 1617.

Gonzales, Franciscus, *Collectio Canonum Ecclesiae Hispanae*,, Matriti: Ex Typographia Regia, 1808.

Jaffé, Phillipus, *Regesta Pontificum Romanorum ab condita Ecclesia ad annum post Christum natum MCXCVIII*, ed. 2, correctam et auctam auspiciis Gulielmi Wattenbach, curaverunt, F. Kaltenbrunner, P. Ewald, S. Loewenfield, 2 vols., 1885-1888.

Labbaeus, Phillipus, S.J., et Cossartius, Gabriel, S.J., *Sacrosancta Concilia*, 15 vols., Lutetiae Parisiorum, 1572.

Mansi, Ioannes, *Sacrorum Conciliorum Nova et Amplissima Collectio*, 53 vols. in 60, Parisiis, Arnhem, Lipsiae, 1901-1927.

Migne, J. P., *Patrologiae Cursus Completus, Series Latina*, 221 vols., Parisiis, 1844-1864.

Potthast, Augustus, *Regesta Pontificum Romanorum inde ab anno post Christum natum MCXCVIII ad annum MCCCIV*, 2 vols., Berolini, 1874-1875.

Turner, Cuthbert, H., *Ecclesiae Occidentalis Monumenta Iuris Antiquissima*, 2 vols., Oxford: Clarendon Press, 1899-1939.

Mediaeval Commentaries

Commentaria in V Libros Decretalium Innocentii IV, Venetiis, 1570.

Hostiensis, *Commentaria in Libros Decretalium*, 6 vols., Venetiis: Apud Iuntas, 1581; et *Summa Aurea*, Venetiis: Ad Candentis Salamandrae Insigne, 1570.

McLaughlin, Terrence, C.S.B., *The Summa Parisiensis*, Toronto: The Pontifical Institute of Mediaeval Studies, 1952.

Schulte, J. Friedrich von, *Die Summa des Paucapalea über das Decretum Gratiani*, Giessen: Verlag von Emil Roth, 1890.

———, *Die Summa Stephanus Tournacensis über das Decretum Gratiani*, Giessen: Verlag von Emil Roth, 1891.

Singer, Heinrich, *Die Summa Decretorum des Magister Rufinus*, Paderborn: Verlag von Ferdinand Schöningh, 1902.

REFERENCE WORKS

Antolin, P., O.S.A., *Catalogo de los Codices Latinos de la Escorial*, 4 vols., Madrid: Imprinta Helenica, 1910.

Barraclough, Geoffrey, *Mediaeval Germany, 911-1250, Essays by German Historians*, 2 vols., Oxford: Basil Blackwell, 1938.

Berardi, Carolus, *Gratiani Canones*, 5 vols., Venetiis: Ex Typographia Petri Valvensis, 1777.

Berger, Adolf, *Encyclopedic Dictionary of Roman Law*, Vol. XLIII, part 2 (1953) of the *Transactions of the American Philosophical Society*, Philadelphia, 1953.

Billot, Louis Cardinal, *De Ecclesia Christi*, 3. ed., Prati: Giachetti, 1909.

Faure, J., *L'Archiprête des Origines au Droit Décrétalien*, Grenoble: Imprimerie-Lithographic Brotel et Guirimand, 1911.

Ferraris, Lucius, *Prompta Bibliotheca Canonica, Iuridica, Moralis, Theologica, necnon Ascetica, Polemica, Rubricistica, Historica*, 9 vols., Romae: Ex Typographia Polyglotta, 1885-1899.

Fournier, Paul, *Les Officialités au Moyen Age*, Paris: E. Plon et Cie., 1880.

Harnack, Adolf, *The Constitution and Law of the Church in the First Two Centuries*, New York: G. P. Putnam's Sons, 1910.

Kober, F., *Die Suspension der Kirchendiener*, Tübingen: Verlag der Buchandlung, 1862.

Kurtscheid, Bertrandus, O.F.M., at Wilches, Felix Antonius, O.F.M., *Historia Iuris Canonici*, Tom. I, *Historia Fontium et Scientiae Iuris Canonici*, Romae: Officium Libri Catholici, 1943.

Lowrie, Walter, *The Church and its Organization in Primitive and Catholic Times*, London: Longmans, Green, and Co., 1904.

Roulers, P. Martinien de, O.M.Cap., *Le Notion de Jurisdiction dans la Doctrine des Décrétistes et des Premiers Décrétalistes de Gratien (1140) a Bernard de Bottone (1250)*, Assisi: Collegio San Lorenzo de Brindisi, 1937.

Schultes, Reginald Maria, O.P., *De Ecclesia Catholica*, Parisiis: P. Lethielleux, 1931.

Schultz, Fritz, *Classical Roman Law*, Oxford: Clarendon Press, 1951.

Sejourné, Paul, *Saint Isidore de Seville: sons rôle dans l'histoire du droit canonique*, Paris: Gabriel Beauchesne, 1929.

Stephenson, Carl, *Mediaeval History*, New York: Harper & Brothers, 1935.

Stickler, Alphonsus, *Historia Iuris Canonici Latini*, Augustae Taurinorum: Apud Custodiam Librariam Pontif. Athenaei Saleciani, 1950.

Stutz, Ulrich, *Die Eigenkirche als Element des mittelalterlich-germanischen Kirchenrechtes*, Berlin: H. B. Müller, 1895.

Van Hove, Alphonsus, *Prolegomena ad Codicem Iuris Canonici*, editio altera et emendatior, Romae: H. Dessain, 1945.

Wernz, Franciscus X., S.J., *Ius Decretalium*, 6 vols., I-II, 3 ed., Prati, 1913-1915.

Wolf, Hans J., *Roman Law*, Norman: The University of Oklahoma Press, 1951.

ARTICLES

Aldama, Jose A. de, S.J., "Indicaciones sobre la cronologia de las obras de S. Isidoro," *Miscellanea Isidoriana*, Romae: Typis Pontificiae Universitatis Gregorianae, 1936, pp. 35-76.

Gallo, Alfonso Garcia, "El Concilio de Coyanza," *Annuario de Historia del Derecho Español*, Tom. XX (1950), pp. 206-347.

Gaudenzi, A., "Il monasterio di Nonantola, il ducata di Persiceto e la chiesa di Bologna," *Bulletino dell' Istituto Storico Italiano*, XXXVII (1916), pp. 107-420.

Kuttner, Stephan, "*Cardinalis*: the history of the canonical concept," *Traditio*, III (1945), pp. 95-184.

Kuttner, Stephan, and Smalley, Beryl, "The *Glossa Ordinaria* to the Gregorian Decretals," *The English Historical Review*, LX (1945), pp. 97-105.

Mollat, G., "Benefices Ecclesiastique en Occident," *Dictionnaire de Droit Canonique*, Vol. III, cols. 406-448, Paris: Libraire Letouzey et Ane, 1937.

Silva- Tarouca, Carlo, S.J., "Nuovi studi sulle antiche lettere dei Papi," *Gregorianum*, XII (1931), pp. 581-603.

Van der Kerckhove, Martin, O.M.Cap., "De notione iurisdictionis apud Decretistas et priores Decretalistas," *Jus Pontificium* XVIII (1938), pp. 10-15.

ABBREVIATIONS

Gonzales—*Collectio Canonum Ecclesiae Hispanae*

JE—Jaffé, *Regesta Pontificum Romanorum* (edited by P. Ewald, for the years 590-882).

JK—Jaffé, *op. cit.* (edited by F. Kaltenbrunner to the year 590).

JL—Jaffé, *op. cit.* (edited by S. Loewenfeld, for the years 882-1198).

Mansi—*Sacrorum Conciliorum Nova et Amplissima Collectio*

MPL—Migne, *Patrologia, Series Latina*

Potthast—*Regesta Pontificum Romanorum, 1198-1304.*

BIOGRAPHICAL NOTE

DONALD EDWARD HEINTSCHEL was born October 24, 1924 at Toledo, Ohio. He attended Saint Louis Parochial School and Central Catholic High School in that city. In September 1942 he entered the University of Toledo and was a student in the pre-medical department of the Arts and Sciences College of this university until June 1944. In September 1944 he entered Saint Peter's Seminary, London, Ontario, Canada. He received a B.A. degree in Honour Philosophy from the University of Western Ontario of which Saint Peter's Seminary is an affiliated college in June 1947. He was ordained to the Holy Priesthood at Toledo on May 19, 1951. In the same month he was assigned as curate at the Queen of the Most Holy Rosary Cathedral in Toledo. In the fall of 1952 he entered the Catholic University of America, where he received the degree of the Baccalaureate in Canon Law in June of the following year, and the degree of the Licentiate in Canon Law in June of 1954.

ALPHABETICAL INDICES

I. Index of Names

II. Index of Subjects

CANON LAW STUDIES*

358. Sesto, Rev. Gennaro J., S.D.B., A.B., S.T.L., J.C.L., Guardians of the mentally ill in ecclesiastical trials.
359. Carroll, Rev. James J., A.B., J.C.L., The bishop's quinquennial report.
360. Curtin, Rev. William Thomas, A.B., J.C.L., The plaint of nullity against the sentence.
361. Ganter, Rev. Bernard J., J.C.L., Clerical attire.
362. Goertz, Rev. Victor M., J.C.L., The judicial summons.
363. Heintschel, Rev. Donald E., A.B., J.C.L., The mediaeval concept of an ecclesiastical office.
364. Kelliher, Rev. Jeremiah F., S.A., A.B., S.T.L., J.C.L., Loss of privileges.
365. Mock, Rev. Timothy, C.M.M., J.C.L., Disqualification of electors in ecclesiastical elections.
366. Smyer, Rev. Francis Anthony, A.B., J.C.L., Canonical regulations regarding exposition of the Blessed Sacrament according to canons 1274 and 1275.
367. Wiggins, Rev. Urban C., A.B., J.C.L., Property laws of the State of Ohio affecting the Church.

* For a complete list of the available numbers of this series apply to the Catholic University of America Press, 620 Michigan Avenue, N.E., Washington 17, D.C., for a general catalogue.

www.ingramcontent.com/pod-product-compliance
Lightning Source LLC
LaVergne TN
LVHW041115090826
844660LV00060B/328

* 9 7 8 0 8 1 3 2 2 5 3 0 2 *